£35.00

THE CREATION OF THE MODERN MINISTRY OF FINANCE IN SIAM, 1885–1910

STUDIES IN THE ECONOMIES OF EAST AND SOUTH-EAST ASIA

General Editors: Peter Nolan, Lecturer in the Faculty of Economics and Politics, University of Cambridge, and Fellow and Director of Studies in Economics, Jesus College, Cambridge, England; and Malcolm Falkus, Professor of Economic History, University of New England, Armidale, New South Wales, Australia

In the last decades of the twentieth century the small- and medium-sized nations of East and South-East Asia have begun a process of potentially enormous political and economic transformation. Explosive growth his occurred already in many parts of the region and the more slowly growing countries are attempting to emulate this vanguard group. The impact of the region upon the world economy has increased rapidly and is likely to continue to do so in the future.

In order to understand better economic developments within this vast and diverse region, this series publishes books on both contemporary and historical issues. It includes works both by Western scholars and by economists from countries within the region.

Published titles include:

Melanie Beresford
NATIONAL UNIFICATION AND ECONOMIC DEVELOPMENT IN VIETNAM

Ian Brown
THE CREATION OF THE MODERN MINISTRY OF FINANCE IN SIAM, 1885–1910

John H. Drabble
MALAYAN RUBBER: THE INTERWAR YEARS

Yujiro Hayami and Toshihiko Kawagoe
THE ACGARIAN ORIGINS OF COMMERCE AND INDUSTRY

Yin-Ping Ho
TRADE, INDUSTRIAL RESTRUCTURING AND DEVELOPMENT IN HONG KONG

Jomo K. S.
GROWTH AND STRUCTURAL CHANGE IN THE MALAYSIAN ECONOMY

Lee Sheng-Yi
MONEY AND FINANCE IN THE ECONOMIC DEVELOPMENT OF TAIWAN

The Creation of the Modern Ministry of Finance in Siam, 1885–1910

Ian Brown
Senior Lecturer in Economic History
with reference to South East Asia
School of Oriental and African Studies
University of London

M

First published 1992 by
THE MACMILLAN PRESS LTD
Houndmills, Basingstoke, Hampshire RG21 2XS
and London
Companies and representatives
throughout the world

ISBN 0–333–54564–8

A catalogue record for this book is available
from the British Library.

Printed in Great Britain by
Ipswich Book Co Ltd
Ipswich, Suffolk

For Manas Chitakasem

Contents

Preface

This book is a revision of a PhD dissertation, 'The Ministry of Finance and the Early Development of Modern Financial Administration in Siam, 1885–1910', which was submitted to the University of London in 1975. In two respects it constitutes a substantial revision. First, it has been considerably cut. Parts of the dissertation have been, or are being, published elsewhere. The details are: 'British Financial Advisers in Siam in the Reign of King Chulalongkorn', *Modern Asian Studies*, 12, 2 (April 1978), pp. 193–215; 'Siam and the Gold Standard, 1902–1908', *Journal of Southeast Asian Studies*, 10, 2 (September 1979), pp. 381–399; 'The End of the Opium Farm in Siam, 1905–07', in John Butcher, Jennifer Cushman and Howard Dick (eds), *The Rise and Fall of Revenue Farming in South-East Asia*, London: Macmillan [forthcoming]. I have not sought to republish those three pieces here, partly because they are easily accessible but principally because each is concerned with a distinct problem, not directly bearing on the central theme of the present book. I have also imposed cuts in another sense – thinning out passages, trimming sentences, in an attempt to correct the extreme wordiness of my earlier self. Second, there is a substantially new conclusion. But in one important respect, the present book has involved no revision of the parent dissertation: I have undertaken no further research, although I have, particularly in the new conclusion, engaged in further reflection. The research for this study, undertaken in Bangkok between April 1971 and July 1972, was made possible by the generous financial assistance of the London – Cornell Project for East and South-East Asian Studies, and of the Thailand National Commission for UNESCO and the Thai Ministry of Education. I received invaluable assistance during my time in Bangkok from Mrs Penporn Satienswasdi of the National Archives and Miss Suchama Dechatiwongse, the Librarian of the Ministry of Finance. In London, at the School of Oriental and African Studies, my work was supervised by Professor C.D.

Cowan, then Professor of the History of South East Asia at the University of London. I received my Thai language instruction, in the academic year 1969/70, from Professor E.H.S. Simmonds, Dr Manas Chitakasem and Mr P.J. Bee. In now preparing the dissertation for publication, the generous assistance of Miss Kanittha Wongpanit of the National Archives enabled me to check my references against the Archives' current indexes. To all, I express my sincere gratitude, and absolve them from responsibility for the final result. I must, as a final comment, return to Dr Manas Chitakasem, one of my Thai teachers in 1969. In the years since then, Dr Manas has continued to give me great assistance, notably in helping to unravel the – to my eyes – more elusive passages in my Thai materials. He, more than anyone, has introduced me to Thai, Thailand and the Thais, and for this, and much friendship, I am extremely grateful. This book is dedicated to him.

School of Oriental and African Studies IAN BROWN
University of London

Notes on Transcription and Chronology

Transcription

In this study, the 'General System of Phonetic Transcription of Thai Characters into Roman' (as set out in the *Journal of the Thailand Research Society*, 33, 1 (March 1941), pp. 49–53) has been employed. There are two exceptions. First, the distinction between long and short vowel is indicated. Second, accepted usage has been followed in the case of some personal names (thus Chulalongkorn rather than Čhulālongkǭn) and in the case of Thai words which have become familiar in English (thus *baht* rather than *bāt*).

Chronology

From the late 1880s to 1911, the Siamese chronological system was the *Rattanakōsinsok* (r.s.), the Bangkok Era (r.s. + 1781 = A.D.). In 1911 it was replaced by the *Phutthasakkarāt* (p.s.), the Buddhist Era (p.s. – 543 = A.D.). In the period covered by this study, the official Siamese year ran from 1 April to 31 March. Thus to convert, for example, the Siamese year r.s. 121 to the Western calendar, it has been necessary to use the cumbersome form 1902/3: p.s. 2456 would be 1913/14.

1 The Setting

1.1 THE IMPERIALIST THREAT AND GOVERNMENT REFORM

In a letter to Prince Damrong, the Minister of the Interior, written in January 1896, King Chulalongkorn of Siam explained the case for the reform of the government administration that had been taking place in the kingdom from the late 1880s.[1] To the west and to the east, the kingdom was faced by European powers whose military strength and systems of administration were much superior to those of the indigenous states they had replaced – and to those of Siam itself. That threat to the independence of Siam could be met, the King argued, by three measures: by maintaining friendly relations with the neighbouring colonial regimes; by possessing sufficient power to maintain the internal peace of the kingdom; and by improving the kingdom's administration to equal that of the European regimes themselves. These measures were inter-dependent. Thus good relations with the powers could not be maintained if the colonial administrations were seriously disturbed by lawlessness in the border areas of Siam. Internal peace and stability depended in turn on the establishment of orderly administration throughout the kingdom. There were further considerations. Under an orderly administration, the people of Siam would have the opportunity and incentive to develop their agricultural and commercial interests. This would increase the government's revenue, which in itself was essential to finance the improvements in administration. And again, the ability of the government to raise revenue required the creation of an effective administrative structure throughout the kingdom: but the establishment and maintenance of that structure depended on the creation of strong government revenues.

Some of these points can be illustrated by the example of the establishment of the Forestry Department in the 1890s. For several decades, British forest companies working in the

Chiangmai area in the north of Siam had been seriously inconvenienced by the arbitrary restrictions placed on their operations by the local chiefs and by an almost intolerable level of lawlessness in the area. At first the companies had complained to the British consul in Bangkok, then after 1884 to a newly-appointed vice-consul in Chiangmai itself. In the early 1890s the Siamese government decided to create a Forestry Department, capable of controlling forestry operations in the north. British forestry experts were to be engaged to train Siamese in modern methods of control and regeneration. It was intended that the establishment of the Department would secure two main benefits. If the Department dealt quickly and effectively with the complaints of the foreign companies, the latter would no longer ask their diplomatic representatives to take up each difficulty with the Siamese authorities: the danger of every problem and set-back suffered by the foresters being transformed by the consul into a political issue would be much reduced. Second, an efficient Forestry Department, responsible to Bangkok, would greatly increase the central government's revenue from the forest fees and duties imposed on the companies. Moreover, by a strictly-enforced restriction on felling and by the introduction of replanting programmes, the government would be able to draw revenue from the northern forests almost indefinitely.[2]

The creation of a Forestry Department capable of efficiently and effectively controlling forest exploitation throughout the kingdom implied a considerable expansion in the central government's responsibilities – and expenditures. Offices and accommodation for officials had to be constructed in the provinces; foreign experts engaged; in the longer term, the government had to meet the costs of training and then maintaining a corps of salaried Siamese forestry officials. The Bangkok government's responsibilities would not rest there. Effective measures against lawlessness could be taken only with the establishment of a permanent police administration in the provinces. The freedom for disgruntled, independent-minded local chiefs to attract the interest of the neighbouring colonial powers, the opportunities for rapacious, oppressive local officials to reduce their domain to anarchy and near-rebellion, could be curbed only through the establishment of a firm, just administration, exercised by government officials loyal and responsible to Bangkok. And again, effective control of the sensitive outer provinces far from the capital depended on the existence of good communications between Bangkok and the border areas – first the telegraph and then the railway. An expanding central and provincial bureaucracy could be staffed with capable officials only if the education system provided a pool for recruitment. A reduction in lawlessness throughout the kingdom, the abolition of extra-territorial privileges for the subjects of the treaty powers, depended significantly on the creation of an efficient judicial structure – and so on. In each case, the government found itself committed to a major increase in its functions and responsibilities – and consequently in its expenditure.

It would be valuable to emphasize the interdependence of the broad measures considered by King Chulalongkorn to be essential for the maintenance of Siamese independence. The orderly administration of the kingdom – on which internal peace depended – necessitated a considerable increase in government expenditure and hence revenue. The latter, in turn, depended on the existence of an administrative structure capable of raising sufficient revenue from the people. Administrative reform and the ability of the government to raise revenue were thus closely bound together. This was particularly so given the fact that under the terms of the commercial treaties signed with the western powers from the mid-nineteenth century – beginning with the Bowring Treaty with Britain in 1855 – Siam was prevented from imposing new taxes on trade and land or from raising the rates on existing ones.[3] As a result, any major increase in revenue could be achieved only through a more efficient exploitation of the existing tax structure – through improved methods of tax administration and collection, particularly in the provinces, and through the development of effective accounting procedures across the administration to ensure that all the revenues collected reached the central treasury.

It should now be evident that the Ministry of Finance, established in 1890 as the ministry responsible for the administration of the government's revenue and expenditure, was at the centre of the reform programmes undertaken by King Chulalongkorn and his ministers. It was the responsibility of the Ministry to see that the revenue was sufficient to finance the schemes, projects and general administration of the government, and to do this by the establishment of a system of tax collection which yielded a large revenue yet was inexpensive to administer and by ensuring that all revenues collected by the various parts of the administration reached the treasury. On the expenditure side, it was the responsibility of the Ministry of Finance to draw up, in consultation with each ministry and department, the budget allocations of the entire administration, to see the budget sanctioned by the Council of Ministers and the King, and finally to ensure that the disbursements of each department from the treasury were in accordance with those allocations.

It should also be evident that the problems to be faced by the Ministry of Finance in carrying out those functions would be partly administrative – how to create a system of financial accountability for both revenue and expenditure for the whole of the central and provincial bureaucracy – but also political – how to persuade, or force, each ministry to accept the authority of the Ministry of Finance in their budget allocation and in the way in which that allocation was used. There would also be sociocultural problems – how to wean officials away from long accepted but now anachronistic conceptions of their functions and responsibilities.

1.2 THE PRE-REFORM ADMINISTRATION

The extent and complexity of those problems can be appreciated only by an examination of the pre-reform structure and system of administration. This subject has already been considered in a number of studies.[4] It is not intended to retrace that ground here but rather to consider only those features of the pre-reform administration which have a direct bearing on the present study.

The basic structure of the pre-reform administration was created by King Trailok in the mid-fifteenth century. At the top were two ministries, the *Mahātthai* and the *Kalāhōm*, which administered the civilian and military populations respectively. Below that, on the civilian side came the four ministries of the *Wang* [Palace], *Nā* [Lands], *Phra Khlang* [Treasury] and the *Nakǫnbān* [Capital]. It would seem that from the first, the financial responsibilities of the *Phra Khlang* [Treasury] were relatively light. Its authority, as for each ministry at that level, extended only to the area immediately surrounding the capital. However, towards the end of the sixteenth century, officials were appointed from the *Phra Khlang* to the provinces, and this increased the flow of revenues to it.[5] Second, major projects initiated by the King – military campaigns, the construction of major temples – were carried out by means of conscripted labour rather than financed from the treasury. As a result, the *Mahātthai* and the *Kalāhōm*, which controlled the corvée, were far more involved in such initiatives than was the *Phra Khlang*.[6]

The financial responsibilities of the *Phra Khlang* were further reduced towards the end of the seventeenth century when, in a major change in the structure of government, the *Mahātthai* and the *Kalāhōm* assumed territorial responsibilities: the *Mahātthai* administered the area to the north of the capital, Ayudhya, the *Kalāhōm* that to the south. The two ministries were responsible for all aspects of administration in their area – the organization of the corvée, justice, the collection of taxes. This implied that the control of the *Phra Khlang* in financial matters – particularly its ability to secure an adequate flow of revenue into the treasury – was still further reduced, for although the authority of the *Phra Khlang* had never extended far beyond the capital, responsibility for tax collections in the provinces now rested firmly with the *Mahātthai* and the *Kalāhōm*.[7]

That the *Phra Khlang* did not disappear altogether was due largely to the fact that from the seventeenth century it began to develop non-financial responsibilities. That period saw a major growth in sea-borne trade between Siam and China, a trade in which vessels prepared on the instructions of the King played a dominant part. The *Phra Khlang* had the task of seeing that the King's ships were loaded with luxury items such as ivory and sapanwood. This task it discharged by collecting *suai* – distinctive products sent to the capital from far distant provinces where, because of the distances involved, the people could not perform corvée labour services for the King. The *Phra Khlang* was also responsible for the distribution within the administration of goods received in return from China. This trade brought the *Phra Khlang* into contact with foreign merchants, and it was therefore inevitable that as increasing numbers of foreigners, including Europeans, came to Siam in the seventeenth century, they came under its jurisdiction. Gradually the *Phra Khlang* began to develop the role of a department of foreign affairs.

However, a more important change in the status and functions of the *Phra Khlang* occurred towards the end of the Ayudhya period. In 1733 King Taisra died, and there followed a brief but very violent succession struggle between his brother and his second son.[8] The throne was won by the brother who became King Boromakot. One of the chief supporters of the defeated second son had been the minister of the *Phra Khlang*, and therefore on ascending the throne King Boromakot promoted one of his own group to that position, at the same time transferring responsibility for the administration of the southern provinces from the *Kalāhōm* to the *Phra Khlang*.[9] The latter now found itself responsible for the administration of justice, the organization of the corvée and the collection of revenue throughout the southern provinces, tasks for which it was largely unprepared and unsuited. Overwhelmed by these new responsibilities, the *Phra Khlang* lost control of virtually all its remaining financial functions. A major part of them – the administration of the King's revenue and expenditure – was transferred to the *Phra Khlang Mahāsombat*, a separate treasury also dating from King Trailok's reforms of the fifteenth century. The preparation of the royal trading ships, which earlier had been entrusted to a subordinate department within the *Phra Khlang*, the *Phra Khlang Sinkhā*, was retained by that department but the department itself now became independent of the *Phra Khlang*. In fact the sole financial responsibility remaining to the *Phra Khlang*, apart from those which arose from the administration of the southern provinces, was the checking of the *bia wat* lists – the annual payments from the King to certain officials. But as the ministry's knowledge of the finances of the administration weakened, so even its control over the *bia wat* deteriorated.[10]

During the reign of Rama I (1782–1809), the administration of the southern provinces was returned to the *Kalāhōm*, with the exception of the eastern gulf region which was retained by the *Phra Khlang* on the grounds that most of the foreigners who came to Siam entered the kingdom through, and carried out their business in, those provinces. In addition, some of the inland provinces under the *Mahātthai* were transferred to the *Phra Khlang*. In effect, the *Phra Khlang* became a third ministry with territorial responsibilities.[11] But although now relieved of some of its territorial functions, there was little possibility that the *Phra Khlang* would regain the limited control over the finances of the administration which it had achieved in the late Ayudhya period. There was almost no possibility that it would develop the control over the flow of revenues and expenditures into and from the treasury that presumably had been envisaged in King Trailok's reforms but never attained. Thus, clearly, the *Mahātthai* and the *Kalāhōm* raised revenue and controlled expenditure in those parts of the kingdom under their administration. Moreover the *Phra Khlang Sinkhā*, although it lost its original function with the decline and later abolition of royal trading from the reign of Rama III (1824–51), greatly increased in importance when it assumed responsibility for the administration of many of the Chinese-run tax farms established during that reign. The *Phra Khlang Sinkhā* also became responsible for the administration of the triennial Chinese poll tax. In fact, according to Prince Damrong, by 1872 ten distinct departments were responsible for the collection of the kingdom's revenues.[12] The crucial point is that each maintained an independent treasury in which their tax collections were held and from which they financed their own administration. The *Phra Khlang Mahāsombat*, which had inherited the financial responsibilities of the *Phra Khlang* towards the end of the Ayudhya period, was but one of those ten departments. It was incapable of forcing the other nine to remit all their tax receipts to the King's treasury; and it was incapable of controlling their expenditures.

In a major speech explaining the reform of the government administration, delivered in the late 1880s, King Chulalongkorn suggested that

> Phrayā Rātchaphakdī [the head of the *Phra Khlang Mahāsombat*] did not know how much revenue would be coming in to finance the government's work. Neither did he have the authority to demand the other departments to remit all their revenue receipts to him. He could only accept whatever they wished to send. Therefore it must be concluded that *the position and the functions of the Phra Khlang did not exist*.... they had been dispersed among the other government departments. As a result, the revenues virtually disappeared. There was not enough for the administration.[13]

Indeed, according to the King, a situation was reached in which the revenues received by the throne fell each year.[14] With regard to the *Phra Khlang* itself, by the nineteenth century it was principally concerned with the administration of the gulf provinces and with the conduct of foreign affairs.

There was a further, political aspect to these developments. From the early Bangkok period through to the 1880s, control of the major ministries was commonly in the hands of one bureaucratic family – the Bunnags.[15] Members of that family, or those closely allied to it, controlled the *Kalāhōm* from 1782 to 1888, and the *Phra Khlang* from 1822 to 1885, except for the years 1865–69. But the Bunnags held numerous important posts throughout the administration. With such a powerful bureaucratic position they were able to divert the revenues collected under their administration away from the King's treasury and towards their own use. Indeed each noble family used its bureaucratic position to increase its own wealth in this way: but the Bunnags, as the dominant family in the administration, were by far the most active. They achieved their greatest influence between 1868 and

1873 when, with King Chulalongkorn still a minor, Čhao Phrayā Sī Suriyawong, the *Kalāhōm* in the reign of Rama IV (1851–68), became Regent, and thus king in all but name.[16] With the throne weak, the ministries were now able to divert a still increasing share of the revenues away from the King's treasury. Chulalongkorn's immediate reaction to that situation is considered below.

The fact that the pre-reform administration could not place at the disposal of the King more than a relatively small proportion of the total revenue raised in the kingdom had a profound influence on the way in which it operated. The most obvious effect, of course, was that the King's ability to finance large-scale expenditures was sharply limited. For the Kings of the Ayudhya and early Bangkok periods, whose active administration of the kingdom was comparatively restricted (in both the geographical and the functional senses), this may not have created too serious a difficulty. But for King Chulalongkorn, who sought to expand the functions and responsibilities of the central government, it clearly was.

A corollary of the financial weakness of the King was that those ministries which collected the kingdom's revenue had a considerable measure of autonomy. As they were not dependent on a central treasury for their resources, they were relatively free to pursue their own interests. There was therefore comparatively little co-operation between ministries unless, of course, two ministries were led by members of one bureaucratic family. The insularity of ministries extended to the point where each had its own facilities for recruiting and training its officials.[17] However not all ministries were well placed to raise revenue. Some did not administer the collection of a lucrative tax or did not provide a service for which they could extract substantial payments from the population. And of course they could not appeal to a central treasury for large funds. As a result, these ministries were starved of resources and were thus unable to carry out their responsibilities effectively. This was the fate of, notably, the various courts of law scattered throughout the administration.[18] In contrast the strong ministries, the *Mahātthai* and the *Kalāhōm*, became stronger, assumed control over increasing numbers of taxes and fees, and over an increasing number of functions and responsibilities. By the Bangkok period they had, in fact, taken on such a heavy burden that their administrative machinery was seriously over-worked. Despite the considerable resources at their disposal, they were weighed down with responsibilities. For both strong and weak ministries, therefore, the result was the same – an inefficient and ineffective administration.[19]

King Chulalongkorn's reform of the government administration, initiated in the late 1880s, was designed to sweep away that system, to create an administrative structure in which each ministry and department had its own firmly defined responsibilities and sufficient resources with which to carry them out.[20] It was further intended that the allocation of resources between ministries would be determined by the government as a whole – the King and the Council of Ministers. An important department would not flounder because of its inability to develop its own sources of revenue.

The nature of the responsibilities of the Ministry of Finance in the reformed administration, and the problems it would face in fulfilling those responsibilities, should now be clear. In essence, each ministry was now required to submit its financial administration, in the immediate perspective, to the Ministry of Finance and, in the wider context, to the government as a whole. They were now required to depend on the Ministry for all their resources and to remit all tax receipts, fees and duties collected under their administration to it. Clearly, that dominance on the part of the Ministry of Finance challenged the well-established financial insularity of ministries and departments. For the period covered by this study, and particularly for the years to 1901 or 1902, here was the major problem for Ministers of Finance.

Turning to consider the ministers and officials themselves, it is important to note that in the pre-reform bureaucracy, salaries were not paid, although officials above a certain level received an annual payment, a royal bounty from the throne – the *bia wat*. Instead officials were expected to retain for themselves a part of the revenues passing through their hands: officials, who took their authority from the King, could extract a portion of the tribute flowing up to the King. This concept of payment was known as *kin mu'ang*, 'to eat the country'. Clearly it had a profound influence on the administrative behaviour of officials. For example, officials and ministers were obviously reluctant to work in those parts of the administration where the opportunities for *kin mu'ang* were small. Those who did work in such departments would strive to retain as much of the limited revenues which passed through their hands as possible; alternatively, in the conduct of their work they would create difficulties in order to force the population to pay for a speedy completion of their business. But even in those departments where the opportunities for *kin mu'ang* were greater, officials would engineer difficulties in order to extract payment; or they would simply neglect those responsibilities which could yield them only a small financial return. Thus, in general, ministers and officials would show enthusiasm only for those projects and tasks in which they could develop a pecuniary interest. Were the King to initiate a measure which held little financial attraction for his officials, each department, by intrigue and complaint, would attempt to pass responsibility to another.[21] It was relatively easy for a department to argue that an unwelcome task could not be its concern, for by the early Bangkok period the functions and duties of departments across the administration had become so confused.

One further aspect of the *kin mu'ang* system requires attention. Government positions, particularly high positions, were regarded primarily as affording the holder an opportunity to maintain his personal standing and wealth. This personal concept of office manifested itself in a number of practical ways. Ministers visited their offices infrequently but commonly conducted their work from their own residences.[22] This, together with the practice of officials retaining a part of the revenues they collected or using the authority of their position to extract financial payments, makes it clear that in the pre-reform administration, no firm distinction could be made between the personal and government activities of ministers and officials. This does not imply that officials paid little attention to the obligations of their office.

There was always the danger that if an official's department became notoriously inefficient or his province was reduced to rebellion by oppression and poor administration, he could well be removed.[23] But, in general, ministers and officials tended to be more concerned with enhancing their personal position, wealth and authority than with the impersonal concepts of governmental responsibility and obligation.

There is a further feature of the pre-reform administration which had a profound effect on administrative behaviour – the existence of a strict bureaucratic hierarchy. Within that hierarchy, an inferior was expected to show deference in speech and behaviour to a superior, never questioning instructions or ideas received, never offering an uncomfortable opinion in return. Were an official to receive instructions which he felt were unacceptable – if, for example, there would be considerable practical difficulties involved in their implementation – then, rather than pointing that out to his superior, the official would simply acknowledge the instructions but then, in some way, avoid carrying them out. Face-to-face confrontation between inferior and superior were to be avoided. A further aspect of this structure was that the superior official simply gave instructions to his subordinate and assumed that they would be carried out. For the former, problems of implementation did not arise.

A less formal structure of relationship within the administration was that of patron–client. These informal alliances between officials commonly cut across the formal hierarchical structure. Thus an official might secure immunity from the control of his formal superior by calling on the protection of his patron, even though the patron was in an administratively unconnected department. In this way patron–client relationships could subvert the formal structure of the administration, as decisions came to be made and actions taken on the basis of informal relationships between officials. In the early reigns of the Bangkok period, into the reign of King Mongkut (1851–68), the hierarchy of patron–client relationships was largely under the control of the Bunnag family.[24] It was the cornerstone of their power. By manipulating those alliances they were able to dominate the administration, to undermine the formal hierarchy of government through which the monarchy expected to operate.

It would be valuable at this point to return to the principal purpose of this section – and place this brief analysis of the pre-reform administration in the context of the governmental reforms undertaken by King Chulalongkorn and, more specifically, the place of the Ministry of Finance in them. It should now be evident that the structure and methods of the pre-reform administration were incompatible with the efficient and effective government of the whole kingdom – it should now be clear why reform was essential. An administrative structure with no strong central financial department was unlikely to be able to mobilize the kingdom's resources in pursuit of effective government from the capital. An administration in which decisions were shaped by informal patron–client relationships, where the division of functions between ministries was severely confused, could hardly be efficient. Efficiency and effectiveness of administration were to be achieved, in essence, by the creation of a functionally-differentiated government structure in which officials had no financial interest in the outcome of their administrative decisions.

The importance of the Ministry of Finance in the reformed administration created by King Chulalongkorn should now also be evident. The Ministry was to be the strong central financial department, receiving into the treasury all the revenues raised in the kingdom, disbursing funds from it to all the divisions of the administration in accordance with agreed allocations. The Ministry was to establish and maintain a system whereby officials would be paid salaries commensurate with their responsibilities and grade, and sufficient to make it no longer necessary for them to resort to *kin mu'ang*. This brief analysis of the pre-reform administration should confirm the difficulties that the Ministry of Finance would face in pursuing those tasks, as at the same time as it was to encourage the emergence of new practices and procedures throughout the administration, those were by no means fully accepted within the Ministry itself. Concepts of administrative and financial propriety developed over centuries were not to be swept aside in the space of two or three decades.

1.3 FINANCIAL REFORM IN THE EARLY YEARS OF THE FIFTH REIGN

Some of the points above can be illustrated by a review of King Chulalongkorn's first attempts at financial reform, undertaken at the end of the regency and in the first years after his accession to full authority. The review will also provide the necessary introduction to the major reforms of the second half of his reign, which is the principal concern of this study.

In the five years of the regency, from 1868 to 1873, the King, and indeed the royal family as a whole, suffered a considerable loss of political and financial power at the hands of the Bunnags. In fact, towards the end of the previous reign, Čhao Phrayā Sī Suriyawong, the future regent, had already transferred the administration of the lucrative spirit farms – and hence their handsome revenues – from the Privy Purse Department to his own ministry, the *Kalāhōm*.[25] During the regency period itself, the Bunnags carried out a number of financial operations which had the effect of reducing still further the flow of revenues to the King and his family.[26] Several princes found themselves in severe financial difficulties.[27] The financial reforms initiated by the King towards the end of the regency period were primarily an attempt to restore the financial, and in turn the political and administrative, power of the crown.

In June 1873 the King issued an edict 'Pertaining to the Financial Department'.[28] It was an uninhibited, almost reckless assault on what the King saw as the failings of the existing financial system – the control of the Bunnag family over sources of revenue (and the power which that control gave them over the informal structure of patron–client relationships within the bureaucracy); the retention of tax revenues within ministries and departments, and the consequent starvation of the treasury and the Privy Purse; the inefficiencies and ineffectiveness of an administration riddled with *kin mu'ang*. The edict created the Finance Office (the *Hǭ Ratsadākǭnphiphat*), a department controlled by the King and independent of the existing government structure. Significantly it was situated within the walls of the Grand

Palace.[29] The kingdom's tax farmers were directed to remit their payments to the new department, the aim being to deprive the ministries of major sources of revenue and to deflect the flow of funds into the treasury. An elaborate system of financial accounts and cross-checks was established to ensure that neither the tax farmers or the officials in the Finance Office had an opportunity to retain part of the funds in their care for their own use. It was made clear that 'the revenue is for the benefit of the State, and not for the benefit of any particular individual.' The edict also included a series of regulations governing the working practices of officials employed in the Finance Office. They were to work regular hours – from 10 a.m. to 4 p.m. They were forbidden to conduct government business in their own homes or indeed in any place other than the Finance Office. Officials were to appoint tax farmers solely on the basis of the highest bid; accepting fees, presents, commission or payment of any kind, or granting privileges or assistance to a farmer were all forbidden. Finally, officials employed in the Finance Office were to receive salaries, so making them financially independent of the conduct of government business.[30] In mid-1874 the newly-established Council of State held a series of meetings to consider further reform of the financial administration.[31] Subsequently a further edict was issued requesting ministries and departments to budget their expenditures in consultation with the Finance Office, and to apply to the latter for permission to undertake any unusual expenditure.[32]

These reforms, although radical in intent, were far from radical in effect. Ironically, the regulations governing the work of officials in the Finance Office did not apply to Prince Mahāmālā, an elderly uncle of the King who had been instrumental in the establishment of the new department and was now its director. Prince Mahāmālā also held a senior position in the Ministry of the Palace where, of course, the old administrative methods were still followed. For this reason he was allowed to continue in the established manner – to work from his residence and to receive commissions and fees. His officials in the Finance Office were, however, expected to comply with the new regulations. Not surprisingly, the new financial and administrative practices maintained only a tenuous existence in the new department; old and new existed side-by-side.[33]

The development of the Finance Office was also hampered by a shortage of qualified and able officials, one so acute that the King feared that the new department would not survive. In 1874 one of its major functions, that of inspecting the administration's revenue and expenditure accounts, was transferred to yet another new department, the Audit Office.[34] This too was independent of the existing administration and situated within the walls of the Grand Palace. In fact it was even more firmly under the control of the King than was the Finance Office. Prince Devawongse, Prince Narēt and Prince Sommot – younger brothers of the King – all found employment there, and the King himself spent a part of each day at work in the department. In time the Audit Office, because of its proximity to the King and the effectiveness of its administration, began to attract other responsibilities, often far removed from its original duties, in the manner characteristic of the pre-reform bureaucracy. Eventually it became the Royal Secretariat, with the task of checking accounts only one of its many duties.[35]

But the major reason why the financial reforms initiated by King Chulalongkorn in the early 1870s failed was that control of the kingdom's revenue remained largely in the hands of the noble bureaucratic families, principally the Bunnags. These families saw to it that not all tax farmers remitted their full payments to the Finance Office,[36] although sufficient revenue was received by it to avert the bankruptcy that earlier had threatened the royal family. In early 1875 the King found it necessary to defend his financial reforms. He pointed out that the government was merely taking steps to ensure that it received the full value of the revenues to which it was entitled and that those revenues were spent wisely. The only people who could object to the reforms were those who had been diverting the revenues into their own pockets. The King emphasized that unless the government received sufficient income it would be unable to maintain expenditure on such vital projects as the improvement of internal communications which would be for the benefit of the people as a whole.[37] Yet the King's explanation could not disguise the fact that his reforms severely challenged the position of the bureaucratic families. In 1874 the Minister of Lands, a nephew of Čhao Phrayā Sī Suriyawong, was dismissed from office on the grounds that he had misused government funds.[38]

Opposition to the King's reforms reached its climax in the so-called Front Palace Incident of December 1874–February 1875.[39] On the night of 28 December 1874, a fire broke out near the gunpowder warehouse within the walls of the Grand Palace. The troops of the Second King, who owed his position to Čhao Phrayā Sī Suriyawong, sought entrance to the Palace, offering their assistance in putting out the blaze. They were refused entry. The Second King then fled and sought refuge in the British Consulate. After considerable negotiation a settlement was reached between King Chulalongkorn and the Second King. The forces of the latter were reduced to a maximum of two hundred men. In return he was granted a larger proportion of the revenues, an indication that the attempted action had been motivated, at least in part, by fear that Chulalongkorn's financial reforms had seriously threatened the sources of income of the Second King and his supporters.

The Front Palace Incident brought the King's reforms to a halt. Indeed Chulalongkorn was so shaken by the strength of the opposition to his measures that he began to purchase property abroad in case he should later need to abdicate and go into exile.[40] But the financial reforms of the early 1870s left an important legacy. The establishment of the Finance Office and of the Audit Office signalled the determination of the King to assume control over the revenues of the kingdom. Although success was limited in this period, for the remaining years of the 1870s and into the 1880s the King maintained some pressure in this area with a series of edicts directing tax farmers and tax officials to remit revenues in full to the treasury.[41] And although the new administrative practices introduced with the establishment of the Finance Office in 1873 never really took root in that department, they were nurtured in the Audit Office/Royal Secretariat in the late 1870s and early 1880s by Prince Devawongse, Prince Narēt and

Prince Sommot. When, in 1885, Prince Devawongse became head of the Department of Foreign Affairs, he introduced into it the reformed methods of financial accounting and correspondence. He was the first Siamese minister to work regular office hours and to receive only a government salary.[42]

As the King's brothers rose to positions of authority in the 1880s, the power of the Bunnag family declined. The ex-regent died in January 1883; in 1885 and 1888 his brother, the *Phra Khlang*, and then his eldest son, the *Kalāhōm*, retired. Those events, together with the death of the Second King in August 1885, allowed King Chulalongkorn to embark on his second and principal period of reform.[43]

It is important to note, however, that although death removed serious political opposition to the King's reforms, many of the bureaucratic attitudes and procedures long practiced by the noble families remained deeply ingrained in the administration. In the late 1880s King Chulalongkorn began to refashion the structure of Siam's government, to create twelve functionally differentiated ministries, including a Ministry of Finance whose responsibility for financial matters was strongly defined. But to infuse that structure with new administrative methods and procedures – to break the commitment of ministries to financial independence, to wean salaried officials away from the behaviour embedded in *kin mu'ang*, to encourage financial co-operation right across the administration to ensure the most effective use of the government's resources – was to prove to be the major problem.

Notes

1. Chulalongkorn to Damrong, 18 January 1896: quoted in Tej Bunnag, *The Provincial Administration of Siam 1892–1915. The Ministry of the Interior under Prince Damrong Rajanubhab*, Kuala Lumpur, 1977, pp. 91–92.
2. Prince Damrong, *Thēsāphibān* [The Thēsāphibān System of Provincial Administration], Bangkok, 1967, pp. 38–41.
3. The provisions of the treaty applied, of course, only to subjects of the treaty power and not to the Siamese themselves. The government of Siam remained free to impose any taxes it wished on its own people. However,

in practice, it was unwilling to make a distinction in this respect between Siamese and European: therefore, in effect, the treaty restrictions on the levying of taxes applied also to the Siamese population.

4. A major work here is H.G. Quaritch Wales, *Ancient Siamese Government and Administration*, London, 1934. Useful analyses are provided by Fred W. Riggs, *Thailand: The Modernization of a Bureaucratic Polity*, Honolulu, 1966; and William J. Siffin, *The Thai Bureaucracy. Institutional Change and Development*, Honolulu, 1966, in both cases as an introduction to an examination of the modern Thai bureaucracy. King Chulalongkorn, 'Phrarātchahatlēkhā phrabāt somdet phra čhunlačhǫmklao čhaoyūhua song thalāeng phraborommarātchāthibāi kāekhai kānpokkhrǫng phāendin' [King Chulalongkorn's Speech Explaining the Changes in the Government], first published in Bangkok in 1927; and Prince Damrong, 'Ru'ang laksana kānpokkhrǫng prathētsayām tāe borān' [The Old System of Government in Siam], both of which are reprinted in *Nangsū' ānprakǫp khambanyāi wichā phū'nthān ārayatham thai* [Handbook on Basic Thai Culture], Thammasat University, 1971, are particularly important. Specific aspects of the pre-reform administration are considered by Wira Wimoniti, *Historical Patterns of Tax Administration in Thailand*, Bangkok, 1961; and Akin Rabibhadana, *The Organization of Thai Society in the Early Bangkok Period, 1782–1873*, Ithaca, 1969.
5. Wales, op. cit., p. 215.
6. King Chulalongkorn, op. cit. [Bangkok, 1927], pp. 5–6.
7. Wales, op. cit., pp. 113–114.
8. W.A.R. Wood, *History of Siam*, London, 1926, pp. 229, 231–232.
9. Neon Snidvongs, 'The Development of Siamese Relations with Britain and France in the Reign of Maha Mongkut, 1851–1868', PhD diss., University of London, 1961, p. 10.
10. King Chulalongkorn, op. cit., pp. 6–7.
11. Neon Snidvongs, op. cit., p. 16.
12. Prince Damrong, 'Tamnān phāsī ākǫn bāngyāng' [The History of Some Taxes], in *Latthi thamniam tāngtāng* [Various Customs], Bangkok, 1963, pp. 176–80.
13. King Chulalongkorn, op. cit., p. 7. Emphasis added.
14. Ibid., p. 42. This is a suitable point to note an important consideration. As King Chulalongkorn was on the point of abolishing the government structure he was describing, some allowance must be made for his probable exaggeration of the failings of the old administration.
15. See David K. Wyatt, 'Family Politics in Nineteenth Century Thailand', *Journal of Southeast Asian History*, 9, 2 (September 1968), pp. 208–28.
16. David K. Wyatt, *The Politics of Reform in Thailand. Education in the Reign of King Chulalongkorn*, New Haven, 1969, pp. 35–62.
17. Siffin, *The Thai Bureaucracy*, p. 34.
18. King Chulalongkorn, op. cit., pp. 21–33; Wales, *Ancient Siamese Government and Administration*, pp. 177–96.
19. King Chulalongkorn, op. cit., p. 56.
20. Ibid., p. 57.

21. Ibid., pp. 56–7.
22. Prince Damrong, *Thēsāphibān*, Bangkok, 1967, p. 11.
23. In this context it is interesting to note that Prince Damrong was the first minister of the *Mahātthai* to undertake regular inspection tours of the provinces. His predecessors had been forced out of the capital only when a crisis in the provinces – a rebellion or the prospect of invasion – had threatened their sources of income or their political position. Prince Damrong, op. cit., p. 24.
24. Akin Rabibhadana, *The Organization of Thai Society in the Early Bangkok Period, 1782–1873*, p. 147.
25. David K. Wyatt, 'The Beginnings of Modern Education in Thailand, 1868–1910', PhD diss., Cornell University, 1966, p. 76, fn. 44.
26. David K. Wyatt, *The Politics of Reform in Thailand*, New Haven, 1969, p. 43.
27. Ibid., p. 53.
28. An English translation of the edict appeared in *Siam Repository*, 4, April 1874, pp. 183–9.
29. *Siam Repository*, 4, January 1874, p. 17.
30. *Siam Repository*, 4, April 1874, pp. 183–9.
31. *Siam Repository*, 4, October 1874, pp. 471–2. The Council of State was established by King Chulalongkorn in May 1874. It was composed of twenty senior officials and members of the royal family, and was to act as an advisory body for the government. David K. Wyatt, *The Politics of Reform in Thailand*, New Haven, 1969, p. 54.
32. Wyatt, op. cit., p. 54.
33. Prince Damrong, *Thēsāphibān*, Bangkok, 1967, p. 11.
34. This department was actually called by the English words 'Audit Office'.
35. Prince Damrong, *Phraprawat somdet phrac̆hao borommawongthōe krom phrayā thēwawong warōpakān* [Biography of Prince Devawongse], Bangkok, 1923, pp. 12–13.
36. Wira Wimoniti, *Historical Patterns of Tax Administration in Thailand*, Bangkok, 1961, pp. 112–14.
37. David K. Wyatt, *The Politics of Reform in Thailand*, New Haven, 1969, p. 57.
38. Ibid., p. 56.
39. For a fuller description and analysis of the 'Front Palace Incident', indeed of this early period of attempted reform as a whole, see Wyatt, op. cit., chap. 2.
40. Wyatt, op. cit., p. 61.
41. Such edicts make up a substantial proportion of the documents concerned with finance from the early part of this reign (the period to the mid-1880s), now held in the National Library.
42. Prince Damrong, *Thēsāphibān*, Bangkok, 1967, p. 12; Prince Damrong, *Phraprawat somdet phrac̆hao borommawongthōe krom phrayā thēwawong warōpakān*, Bangkok, 1923, p. 20.
43. Wyatt, op. cit., pp. 84–5.

2 The Early Years of the Ministry of Finance: its Establishment and Collapse, 1885–96

In 1885 Prince Mahāmālā, the head of the *Hǭ Ratsadākǭnphiphat* (the Finance Office) from its establishment in the early 1870s, retired. He was succeeded first by his nephew, Prince Čhakkraphatdiphong, and then, when Prince Čhakkraphatdiphong became ill, by another of King Chulalongkorn's brothers, Prince Narāthip Praphanphong.[1] It was Prince Narāthip, at that time in his mid-twenties,[2] who was to guide the establishment of the modern Ministry of Finance and the introduction of the first financial reforms of Chulalongkorn's second reform period.

2.1 PRELUDE TO THE ESTABLISHMENT OF THE MINISTRY OF FINANCE: THE FINANCE OFFICE AND REVENUE, 1885–90

Until the establishment of the Ministry of Finance in October 1890, Prince Narāthip was simply the head of the Finance Office. As such his principal responsibility was to ensure that the revenues collected by the various ministries and departments were remitted in full to the treasury. In the mid–1880s many, if not most of the taxes imposed in the kingdom remained under the control of departments other than the Finance Office. However in 1886 an undertaking was obtained from the minister of the *Kalāhōm*, Čhao Phrayā Surawong Waiyawat, the eldest son of the ex-regent, that in future all revenues collected under his administration would be forwarded in full to the Finance Office, and furthermore, that the Finance Office would supervise the auctions for all tax farms attributed to the *Kalāhōm*.[3] Over the following few years Prince Narāthip appointed groups of officials to the Finance Office, each group taking responsibility for the revenues received into the treasury from one particular ministry. They were responsible for exerting pressure on that ministry not to fall into arrears, for checking monies received and for preparing accounts.[4] In 1888 six officials were appointed to check the overall flow of revenues into the treasury.[5] It is evident that with the waning of the power of the Bunnag family in the 1880s, the Finance Office under Prince Narāthip was in a much stronger position to increase the volume of revenues reaching the treasury than had been the case under Prince Mahāmālā in the early 1870s, when the Bunnags had been at the height of their power. Nevertheless it is interesting to note that when, in 1886, the *Kalāhōm* agreed to remit its revenues in full to the treasury, it was still under the control of a Bunnag.

In the late 1880s Prince Narāthip also introduced a number of measures to strengthen the administration's control over, and thus its income from, the three main revenue farms in the kingdom – the spirit, gambling and opium monopolies.[6] The administration was particularly concerned about the opium farm. In the first place, it was the most profitable of the three main monopolies; in 1889/90 it yielded 2 million *baht*,[7] approximately 15 per cent of the government's total revenue. More importantly, by the late 1880s the operation of the opium monopoly had become so demanding that only the richest Chinese syndicates had the resources to take it on. Indeed by that time a major proportion of the opium sales in the kingdom was controlled by just one syndicate. In 1890 a separate syndicate was created merely to administer the retail sales in Bangkok's twelve hundred-odd opium shops.[8]

This heavy concentration of power had two main consequences, both damaging to the government's interest. As the wealth and power of the opium farmers grew, so, paradoxically, their position became more precarious. The profits to be made from the farm, the patronage associated with the position of opium farmer, produced intense rivalry between the syndicates competing for control of the monopoly, a rivalry heightened by the fact that the syndicates were closely associated with the Chinese secret societies.[9] As the government was dependent on the one syndicate for a considerable part of its opium revenue, the collapse of the syndicate as a result of the machinations of its rivals would have the most damaging impact on the government's income. Second, and as an alternative, it was possible that with few syndicates in a position to bid for the opium contract, the farmers, instead of competing against each other would come to an understanding among themselves that would allow each to hold the contract in turn. In this way, the syndicates would reduce the price of the farm – the government's revenue – and increase their own profits.

In 1889 King Chulalongkorn established a committee under the chairmanship of Prince Devawongse, and including Prince Narāthip and Čhao Phrayā Rattanabǫdin, to examine the structure and operations of the opium monopoly.[10] The committee's report formed the basis for a 'Supplementary Law Relating to the Opium Monopoly', which came into operation in April 1890.[11] Under this legislation, responsibility for the monopoly, which had been held by the *Kalāhōm* from the Fourth Reign, passed to the Ministry of Finance. This is the clearest example of the way in which, in the late 1880s, the major ministries in the pre-reform administration were releasing their control over the kingdom's revenues to a centralized finance department. The first auctions under the new legislation were held in late March 1890, and resulted in a substantial increase in the government's revenue from the monopoly.[12]

With respect to the gambling farms, in 1888 the government closed every small gambling den in Bangkok Province (some 277 premises) and reduced the number of larger dens from 126 to 67.[13] By 1893 only 16 dens remained in the area of the capital. Over the same period the authorities introduced strict regulations to govern the operations of the remaining dens.[14] These reforms were carried through without causing a fall in the revenue from gambling – indeed quite the reverse. Improved methods of administration, tighter control over the operations of the den managers, allied to the fact that increased business at the remaining dens compensated for the revenue lost by the closing of the smaller ones, ensured a considerable increase in government revenue from this source.[15]

With respect to the kingdom's spirit farms, Prince Narāthip took the following action. By an 'Internal Taxation Law' in 1886 and an 'Excise Law' in 1887, he codified and restated the existing legislation governing the operation of the spirit farm contracts,[16] in an attempt to enforce the law as it stood. Then, from 1889, provincial authorities were instructed to carry out raids against illicit stills in their area, [17] as the production of the latter was a major threat to the business of the spirit farmers and thus to the expansion of the government's spirit revenue. Finally, also in 1889, responsibility for the collection of the import duty on foreign spirits, until then entrusted to the spirit farmers, was transferred to the Customs Department.[18] This was an early example of one of the most important financial reforms of this whole period – the gradual abolition of the system of revenue farming and the expansion of tax collection by government officials.

Prince Narāthip's measures to increase the flow of revenues into the treasury – the introduction of stricter control over the opium, spirit and gambling monopolies, and the imposition of more effective pressure on the other ministries to yield up their full revenue receipts – met with considerable success. In 1886 there was a sudden doubling of treasury revenues over the figure for 1885, and the new level was maintained for the rest of the decade.[19] By 1890 the treasury was assured of a substantially greater and more reliable flow of funds. With the formal establishment of the Ministry of Finance in that year, attention could focus on the distribution of those resources throughout the administration – on the problem of controlling government expenditure.

2.2 THE ESTABLISHMENT OF THE MINISTRY OF FINANCE IN 1890

It was also in the late 1880s that Prince Narāthip began the reorganization of the various financial departments of the government –

gathering the financial functions of the administration into a rapidly expanding Finance Office, in preparation for the formal establishment of the Ministry of Finance. This reorganization reached fruition in October 1890 when, on the promulgation of the 'Act Concerning the Functions of the Ministry of Finance', the Ministry finally came into being.[20] In the opening words of the Act, the Ministry of Finance was to be responsible for 'receiving, disbursing and maintaining the whole income and treasure of the government, for maintaining accounts, and for collecting the taxes throughout the whole kingdom'.[21] The Ministry was divided into thirteen departments [*krom*], which in turn fell into three groups. First there were five administrative departments: *Krom Phra Khlang Klāng* [the Central Office]; *Krom Sārabānchī* [Accounts Department]; *Krom Truat* [Investigation Department]; *Krom Kep* [Treasury]; and the *Krom Phra Khlang Khāngthī* [the Privy Purse Department]. Then there were five taxation departments: *Krom Suai* [Capitation Tax Department]; *Krom Sanphākǫn* [a taxation department, responsible mainly for the spirit, gambling and opium monopolies]; *Krom Sanphāsī* [another taxation department]; *Krom Thī Din* [Land Tax Department]; and the *Krom Sunlakākǫn* [Customs Department]. Finally there were three production departments: *Krom Krasāpsithikān* [the Mint]; *Krom Kānphimbat* [Printing Department]; and the *Krom Rātchaphatsadu* [a purchasing and sales department].

The 1890 Act went through each of the thirteen departments of the Ministry, laying down the number of senior officials that there would be in each department, their rank and their responsibilities. It is important to note that the Act also instructed the Ministry's officials to bring to the attention of their superior any error that he, the superior, may have made: and if the Minister himself was at fault, his officials were to place the matter before the King. Senior officials were assured that their Minister would be unable to dismiss them without the prior sanction of the King.[22] Such instructions and assurances represented a firm break with the practices of the traditional bureaucracy.

This principal act was rapidly followed by a number of smaller pieces of legislation dealing in detail with the responsibilities of the constituent departments of the Ministry. For example, that same month, October 1890, saw the promulgation of the 'Privy Purse Department Act'.[23] The Act involved an attempt to define more clearly a distinction between the finances of the King and the finances of the state. Such a distinction had little meaning in the old system of government where, in theory at least, every object in the domain was in the King's possession. However, at some point either in the late Ayudhya or the early Bangkok period, the King had established a separate treasury, adjacent to the Throne Room, from which he could make disbursements without the knowledge of his officials. Rama III (1824–1851) had greatly increased the size of this treasury, and in the following reign, the *Phra Khlang Khāngthī*, or Privy Purse Treasury, had been created. As the importance of this separate treasury in the expenditure of the King grew, a distinction between the finances of the crown and the finances of the state began to develop. For example, in the reign of King Mongkut (1851–1868), a number of residences were constructed for members of the royal family. Construction was financed by the *Phra Khlang Khāngthī*, and as a result the residences were considered the property not of the government but of their occupants.[24] The Privy Purse Act of 1890 further developed the distinction.

Prior to 1890 the Privy Purse, like all the major departments in the administration, had attributed to it a number of revenue farms and other sources of income. Revenue receipts from those sources were sent to the department: a proportion was retained for the personal use of the King, and the remainder was remitted to the treasury. The 1890 Act stipulated that all revenues received by the Privy Purse, including rent on property owned by the King and interest and profit on the King's financial transactions, were to be remitted in full to the treasury.[25] In return, each year the Privy Purse would be allocated 15 per cent of the government's total revenue. It was further decreed that, as the Privy Purse was now a department within the Ministry of Finance, it would maintain accounts of all its transactions and submit them, monthly, for examination by the Accounts Department of the parent ministry. Only in strictly private matters – for example if the King were to make payments to a member of his immediate family – was the Privy Purse independent of the Ministry of Finance.

A second example of supporting legislation was the act for the *Krom Kep*, promulgated in December 1890.[26] As the department was responsible for holding the government's revenues and treasure, the act was primarily concerned with establishing firm standards of financial propriety for its officials. It strongly stated that as the latter now received a government salary, they were strictly forbidden from accepting or taking any other remuneration that might arise in the course of their work. A long list of detailed regulations was provided, covering virtually every transaction within the department, in an attempt to ensure that all monies were accounted for at all times, so that officials would find it extremely difficult to divert revenues into their own pockets. Similar regulations were created for each department of the Ministry of Finance.[27]

2.3 THE BEGINNING AND FAILURE OF BUDGETARY CONTROL 1890–93

The establishment of the basic structure and responsibilities of the Ministry of Finance in 1890 enabled Prince Narāthip to proceed, towards the end of 1891, with the first attempt to produce a revenue and expenditure budget, in preparation for the formal inauguration of the reformed government structure the following April, the beginning of the Siamese year.[28] Certainly the Ministry of Finance proved capable of providing figures for the principal heads of revenue and expenditure for the year 1892/3, although it is impossible to judge how accurate the figures were.[29] Yet it would appear that this first budget was not produced without creating considerable friction between Prince Narāthip and his ministerial colleagues.

At the root of this conflict was the fact that the Council of Ministers, formally inaugurated in April 1892, was unwilling, perhaps unable, to devise procedures for resolving inter-ministerial disputes to arrive at agreed priorities. To a considerable extent the disunity within the Council derived from the fact that in mid-1892 the King had withdrawn from the immediate affairs of government, hoping to pass the burden of daily administration to his ministers and leave himself responsible only for the broad direction of policy. During the following few months he spent an increasing time at Kọ Si Chang, an island in the Gulf of Siam.[30] The removal of the King's steadying influence and experience proved fatal. Sir Henry Norman, who was then in Bangkok, described the activities of the Council of Ministers in 1892/3 as 'a nine months' carnival of intrigues and jealousies, followed by a three months' nightmare of cabals and recriminations'.[31] In such an atmosphere it was clearly very difficult for the Ministry of Finance to impose control over the total level of government expenditure or over the expenditure allocations of the various ministries and departments.

However Prince Narāthip's response to this situation undoubtedly made the task of the Ministry considerably more difficult. In deciding the expenditure allocations of the government, his basic approach was to refuse any new or unusual outlay.[32] As long as total expenditure was covered by the year's revenue he was not particularly concerned about the expenditure distribution between the ministries. For example, when, in early 1892, the commander of the army, Čhao Phrayā Surasakmontrī, presented a request for new equipment and uniforms for his troops, it was refused out of hand by Prince Narāthip with the comment that 'nowadays the whole world has stopped using weapons of war and has taken to the pen instead'.[33] In the circumstances such blunt, indiscriminate tactics may have been the only means by which some control over total expenditure could be maintained. But inevitably those tactics strengthened the determination of the ministers to escape or subvert the control of the Ministry of Finance.

Ministers could achieve this either by ignoring the expenditure estimates or by retaining some of the revenues still collected under their administration. Indeed, in this period the practice developed of ministries holding part of their funds with the newly-established Bangkok branch of the Hongkong and Shanghai Bank, out of sight of the Ministry of Finance.[34] In response Prince Narāthip attempted with increasing determination to ensure that the full tax revenues were forwarded to the treasury.[35] In 1891 he circulated a memorandum which stated that any official discovered holding back the revenues in his care would be severely punished;[36] in June 1892 the King himself wrote to the Council of Ministers to urge each minister to forward all revenues collected under their authority to the treasury.[37]

Prince Narāthip antagonized his ministerial colleagues in another way. In a situation where almost every ministry had a list of projects which it was eager to implement but where those ambitions were commonly frustrated by the parsimonious attitude of the Ministry of Finance, it was quickly noted that the Ministry of Finance itself always appeared to have adequate resources for its own schemes. There was little evidence that Prince Narāthip was willing to impose the same austerity on his own ministry that he was so eager to impose on those of his colleagues.

Three of Prince Narāthip's projects stood out as particular objects of controversy, and perhaps envy. He proposed the introduction of a government paper currency, which involved ordering some four million currency notes from Europe in late 1890.[38] As part of a series of measures designed to improve the efficiency of the government mint, Prince Narāthip proposed ordering modern *baht*-minting and copper-coin minting machinery from Europe to replace the existing equipment which had been installed over thirty years earlier.[39] Finally the Minister embarked on a series of tax reforms, including the introduction of more effective procedures for the collection of the triennial Chinese poll tax,[40] and the introduction of measures to increase the proportion of government revenue collected by officials,[41] which inevitably involved a substantial increase in the staff of the Ministry of Finance – and thus in the Ministry's expenditure. Indeed with the formal establishment of the Ministry in 1890, Prince Narāthip quickly made a considerable number of appointments in all departments. In December 1891 additional officials were engaged to work on the budget;[42] still more were recruited the following month; [43] the staff of the Customs Department was increased in March 1892;[44] new appointments were made to the Accounts Department in late

1892.[45] It would appear that in just the two years from April 1890 to April 1892, the number of officials employed in the Ministry of Finance virtually doubled:[46] over the same period, the expenditure of the Ministry may well have increased by a similar degree.[47]

At a time when the expenditure allocation of each ministry depended to a considerable extent on the ability of its minister to dominate in the 'carnival of intrigues and jealousies' taking place in the Council, inevitably there was resentment at the success of any individual who secured resources for his proposals. But the resentment felt against Prince Narāthip was particularly strong. As Minister of Finance he was striving to achieve control over the government's revenue resources, and therefore, by implication, was moving towards the position where he could assert a dominating influence over the expenditure of all ministries. In addition, there was a strong suspicion among his colleagues that not only was Prince Narāthip securing almost all the budget allocations proposed for his own ministry but that those proposals were in themselves frequently extravagant.

2.4 THE RESIGNATION OF PRINCE NARĀTHIP, MARCH 1893

The conflict between Prince Narāthip and his colleagues came to a head early in 1893. In late February and early March, Prince Narāthip submitted to the King the detailed expenditure estimates of the government for the year 1893/4.[48] It was the Prince's hope that in that year a considerable proportion of the revenue – apart from that derived from the major spirit, gambling and opium monopolies – would be collected by officials rather than farmed out. Consequently the estimates for his own ministry included very substantial increases – in some cases a doubling – in the expenditures of the revenue departments, particularly for the *Krom Sanphāsī* and the *Krom Sanphākǫn*.[49] However, because the officials in the revenue departments would take some time to become proficient in the assessment and collection of taxes,

Prince Narāthip calculated that the revenues collected by those departments in 1893/4 would be lower than the revenues received from the corresponding tax farmers in 1892/3. Although there appears to have been some support in the Council for Prince Narāthip's basic position, it was strongly felt that his expenditure estimates were extravagant. Under pressure, the Minister agreed to a small reduction in the expenditure allocation for the *Krom Sanphāsī*.[50] There was deadlock. The King then appointed a committee, led by Prince Devawongse and including Prince Damrong, Prince Phānuphanwong, Prince Narit and Prince Svasti,[51] to examine the expenditure estimates for the *Krom Sanphāsī* and the *Krom Sanphākǫn*. The committee found Prince Narāthip's estimates to be extravagant, and imposed large cuts.[52]

But that was not the end of the matter. While examining the accounts of the revenue departments, Prince Devawongse's committee came across evidence of extravagance and mismanagement in other parts of the Ministry of Finance, and, with the approval of the Council of Ministers, proceeded to a detailed investigation of the accounts of the Central Office, the Accounts Department, the treasury and the mint.[53] Following that investigation, the committee recommended some minor changes to the structure of the Ministry of Finance, changes that would strengthen the Ministry's audit and accounting procedures and reduce the number of its officials. The committee also proposed that the foreign orders for new machinery for the mint be substantially reduced, and that the paper currency scheme be dropped.

But there was a more disturbing issue. During the course of its investigations, Prince Devawongse's committee came across numerous discrepancies in the accounts of some departments. For example, each of the monthly accounts of the opium revenue for the year 1892/3 failed to balance.[54] The committee was drawn towards the conclusion that substantial misappropriation was taking place within the Ministry of Finance. Perhaps the most serious suspicions concerned the Privy Purse. In the early 1890s ill-health had forced the head of the Privy Purse Department to hand over his responsibilities to his ministerial superior, Prince Narāthip.[55] As Minister of Finance, Prince Narāthip already had some responsibility for the accounts of wives and children of the King held at the Hongkong and Shanghai Bank in Bangkok. These accounts were usually held in trust in the names of Prince Narāthip and Prince Sommot, the King's secretary. It was now suspected that Prince Narāthip had misled Prince Sommot and withdrawn funds on his own initiative, although how those funds had then been used was never stated.[56]

The anger of the Council of Ministers engulfed Prince Narāthip. He was subjected to a stream of accusations which culminated, on 16 March 1893, in a demand from the Minister of Agriculture, Čhao Phrayā Surasakmontrī, that he be dismissed.[57] On that occasion Prince Narāthip was saved by the intervention of Prince Devawongse. But within a few days, as Prince Devawongse continued his investigation, he too became convinced that malpractice had taken place. On 20 March he wrote to the Hongkong and Shanghai Bank, instructing it not to allow Prince Narāthip to draw on the accounts held in his name, unless permission had been given by Prince Sommot.[58] That same day he wrote to the King to call for Prince Narāthip's dismissal: to allow him to resign would constitute insufficient punishment.[59]

In two letters to the King, Prince Narāthip strongly denied that he was guilty of malpractice.[60] He argued that the discrepancies discovered in the accounts of his ministry had arisen without his knowledge or involvement. He also argued that the earlier charges of extravagance laid against him could not be sustained, as all the expenditure allocations of the Ministry of Finance had been approved by the Council of Ministers and by the King himself. Prince Narāthip then drew the King's attention to the achievements of the Ministry of Finance under his direction, particularly its success in increasing the flow of revenues into the treasury. But he also asked the King for permission to resign. This was not, he emphasized, an admission of guilt. He simply needed to escape from the hostility that now surrounded him. His request was granted. On 21 March 1893 Prince Narit, who had been Minister of Public Works since 1889, became Minister of Finance. Prince Sommot became Director of the Privy Purse Department.[61] Prince Narāthip never again held a ministerial position.[62]

On balance it would appear that the allegations of impropriety levelled against Prince Narāthip provided merely the immediate circumstances of his downfall, but were not the primary cause. In this context it is important to note that the minister who had demanded the resignation of Prince Narāthip at the meeting of the Council on 16 March 1893, Čhao Phrayā Surasakmontrī, had earlier, as commander of the army, been refused an increased expenditure allocation by the Minister of Finance. Revenge may have been in Čhao Phrayā Surasakmontrī's mind in March 1893. And it is surely significant, and certainly ironic, that within a short time Čhao Phrayā Surasakmontrī himself was accused of the unauthorized use of funds and yet was allowed to clear his name and retain his ministerial position.[63]

2.5 PRINCE NARIT AS MINISTER OF FINANCE, 1893–94

The resignation of Prince Narāthip pushed the Council of Ministers towards complete disintegration. By the time the crisis with France, which had been gathering with a series of border incidents in early 1893, finally broke in July, the Council was incapable of effective administration. It was largely through the adroit diplomacy of Prince Devawongse, working independently of the Council, that the political sovereignty of Siam was preserved, although at considerable cost. Siam was forced to cede all territory on the east bank of the Mekong, withdraw her forces to a distance of 25 kilometres from the west bank, evacuate the provinces of Battambang and Siemrap and pay an indemnity of three million francs. The French were to occupy Chantabun until Siam evacuated the east bank of the Mekong.[64]

The territorial losses suffered by Siam, together with the collapse of the Council of Ministers, brought King Chulalongkorn close to a physical and nervous breakdown which, in effect, removed him from administration.[65] Inevitably the machinery of government almost ceased to function. After August 1893 the Council of Ministers no longer met.[66] Some ministries were able to ride this collapse and continue reforms begun in the earlier period – notably the Ministry of the Interior, which pressed ahead with its reorganization of provincial administration, and the Ministry of Foreign Affairs, which had to deal with the French crisis – through the resourcefulness and independence of their ministers, Prince Damrong and Prince Devawongse. But those ministries which lacked an energetic head and where there was little reform momentum (and this included the Ministry of Finance) slipped towards inactivity, for the King had neither the physical or mental strength, or the interest, to sustain their work.

But in the years immediately following the collapse of the Council, the Ministry of Finance bore a further handicap – the antagonism felt across the administration at its earlier attempts to impose financial control. There could be no question of the Ministry of Finance tackling that crucial issue until the King had returned to the centre of the government and until the Council of Ministers had been resurrected and was operating in an effective manner. Consequently, for the short period for which Prince Narit was Minister of Finance, March 1893 to December 1894, the Ministry was almost dormant.

A skeleton set of revenue and expenditure estimates for 1893/4, prepared by Prince Narāthip and amended by Prince Devawongse's committee, was inherited by Prince Narit. But there is little indication that the ministries attempted to abide by those allocations or that Prince Narit attempted to enforce them. The Ministry of Finance prepared a rough budget for 1894/5, and despite the difficulties involved in convening a meeting of the ministers to consider it,[67] and the King's continuing indisposition, it appears to have been discussed and sanctioned. However, that 1894/5 budget then became a deadletter, for a number of ministries appear to have operated without approved funds for that year.[68] They were forced to work outside the budget, to finance themselves by retaining a proportion of the revenues collected under their authority and by maintaining undisclosed accounts at the Hongkong and Shanghai Bank.[69] It would be no exaggeration to say that in the period when Prince Narit was Minister, the Ministry of Finance exerted almost no control over the finances of the government.

The Ministry's weakness revealed itself in other ways. In March 1893 the opium farm contracts came up for re-sale; but in the confusion of the time no auction was held for many of the principal farms.[70] A short time later two tax farmers, Phra Phakdīphatarākǫn and Phra Čharoenrātchathǫn, approached the Ministry of Finance, offering to administer the opium monopoly throughout virtually the whole kingdom.[71] The Ministry agreed.[72] Indeed it would appear that the Ministry of Finance was willing to transfer control over almost all aspects of the monopoly to Phra Phakdīphatarākǫn and Phra Čharoenrātchathǫn, for the latter were allowed to buy the government's stock of raw and prepared opium.[73] In effect, from mid-1893 government control over the activities of the opium farmers was reduced to periodic inspections of their accounts by the *Krom Sārabānchī*. It would seem that this abrogation of responsibility on the part of the Ministry of Finance – against the requirements of the 1890 opium law – arose from the fact that the Ministry, shaken by its severe internal crisis, feared that it would now be unable to administer the monopoly effectively. The offer by Phra Phakdīphatarākǫn and Phra Čharoenrātchathǫn was seen as the only way in which the government's revenue from opium might be maintained. An alternative explanation is that the Ministry of Finance, its administrative machinery in ruins, simply lost control of the situation.

Indeed in the otherwise rather barren period of Prince Narit's tenure at the Ministry, only two positive features stand out. In November 1893 the Privy Purse Department was removed from the Ministry of Finance and placed in the Ministry of the Privy Seal. Prince Sommot was confirmed as Director of the Department.[74] Second, Prince Narit, like Prince Narāthip, was anxious to increase the proportion of revenue collected by government officials. Although Prince Narāthip's expenditure allocations for the *Krom Sanphāsī* and *Krom Sanphākǫn* had been a principal cause of the crisis which had eventually led to his resignation, Prince Devawongse's committee, investigating the Ministry's accounts in 1893, had in fact been prepared to accept significant increases in the expenditure budgets of those two departments.[75] The result was that, with increased resources, the

Krom Sanphāsī almost doubled its revenue receipts in 1893/4 over the preceding year.[76] The department became responsible for the administration of the Chinese poll tax in 1894, a year in which a record number of Chinese were taxed.[77] Indeed, it must be noted that, despite the virtual collapse of budget and accounting procedures, the value of revenue flowing into the treasury was maintained, [78] although it should be added that the kingdom was now enjoying a trade boom, after a pronounced commercial depression in the first years of the decade.

In the second half of 1894 the King's physical and mental condition improved, although even at the end of that year his recovery was still not complete.[79] There were now indications that attempts would soon be made to reorganize the administration and to repair the damage which had been caused by the internal and external crises of 1892–1893.[80] It was in this context that at the end of December 1894 Prince Narit was transferred to the Ministry of War, [81] and Prince Sirithat Sangkāt became Minister of Finance, his first ministerial appointment. He was the third Minister of Finance in the four years since the Ministry had been formally established.

2.6 PRINCE SIRITHAT SANGKĀT AS MINISTER OF FINANCE, 1894–96

Prince Sirithat was to remain at the Ministry of Finance for less than two years. But in that time he made a determined effort to revive the Ministry after the collapse of 1893 and to overcome the inactivity which had then taken hold under Prince Narit. A major failure of Prince Narit's period of office had been the Ministry's virtual relinquishment of control over the administration of the opium monopoly, and it is therefore significant that one of the first concerns of Prince Sirithat on his appointment was to attempt to regain that control. By 1895 relations between the government and the Phra Phakdīphatarākǫn-Phra Čharoenrātchathǫn syndicate, which had controlled virtually all opium sales in the kingdom since mid-1893, were extremely poor. For example, in

1894 the syndicate and the administration were in conflict over a proposed increase in the permitted retail price of opium.[82] In such a dispute the government was at a considerable disadvantage, for the opium monopoly accounted for some 15 percent of its total revenue, and it was largely in the hands of that single syndicate. In mid-1895 Prince Sirithat and the King decided that, on re-auction, the monopoly would again be divided into a number of smaller, separate farms, thereby reducing the power of each opium farmer.[83] They also agreed that in order to reassert the government's control over the supply of opium, the Customs Department would become responsible for the import of raw opium and for its distribution, in strictly regulated quantities, to the farmers.[84]

But undoubtedly the most important initiative of Prince Sirithat's short term as Minister of Finance was his attempts to compile a revenue and expenditure budget for the government. During the opening months of 1895 the Minister held discussions with some of his ministerial colleagues over their estimates for the coming year. But by 15 March, the date by which the Ministry of Finance was expected to submit the full estimates to the King, those discussions were far from complete.[85] It was not until October that the full estimates were sent to the King for his approval – over six months behind schedule.[86] The King sanctioned the budget but suggested to Prince Sirithat that if his officials began work immediately on the budget for the coming year, that would start in April 1896, then perhaps those estimates would be completed on time.[87] Prince Sirithat wrote immediately to each of the ministers, asking them to submit their preliminary expenditure estimates to him no later than 15 December 1895. But by that date only the Royal Secretariat, the Privy Purse Department and the Police Department had complied with his request.[88] In January 1896 Prince Sirithat sent warning letters to the remaining ministries but only the Ministry of Agriculture responded.[89] By March estimates had been received from the Ministry of the Capital and the Ministry of Public Works,[90] but there was still nothing from the ministries under Prince Damrong, Prince Devawongse and Prince Narit. As the new financial year approached, the King wrote in strong terms to those ministers who had failed to comply with the requests of the Ministry of Finance.[91] Most of the remaining ministerial estimates were in by the end of May: but by the time Prince Sirithat left the Ministry in August 1896, those of the Ministry of War and of the Ministry of Foreign Affairs and still to come before the Council of Ministers.[92] In short, Prince Sirithat, like Prince Narāthip before him, had failed to establish the procedures and mechanisms of budgetary control.

There were obvious dangers in such a situation. In the period 1892–1896 each ministry had sought large expenditure allocations, with little regard for the requirements of the government as a whole. Ministers had consistently failed to co-operate with each other in producing an agreed order of priorities for government expenditure.[93] Inevitably some potentially important initiatives had thus been ignored, some less vital projects had been sanctioned. There was a further danger. Unless the ministries co-operated with each other in drawing up the expenditure estimates, there was every likelihood that total expenditures would soar above total revenue.

2.7 1896: A NEW MINISTER OF FINANCE AND THE APPOINTMENT OF A FINANCIAL ADVISER

Perhaps it was asking too much of the Ministry of Finance to develop as an effective and influential component of the government during the period of severe political and administrative instability that afflicted Siam in the first half of the 1890s. In other words, an influential Ministry of Finance could establish itself only in the context of a stable political environment, and that in turn depended to a considerable extent on the exercise of firm leadership by the King. It is therefore not surprising that when King Chulalongkorn resumed his dominant position in the administration in the course of 1896, important changes should take place at the Ministry of Finance.

The first concerned the appointment of a European financial

adviser. As far back as April 1890, Prince Narāthip had suggested that, in view of the lack of financial expertise within the administration, a European adviser should be appointed,[94] but nothing had come of this. The issue was revived in late 1894 or in early 1895 by the government's General Adviser, Rolin Jacquemyns, who argued that a European financial adviser could assist in the reform of the administrative procedures of the Ministry of Finance and with the publication of the government's annual budget, which would be vital in establishing Siam's financial credit in the world.[95] He made it clear that the financial adviser

> should be appointed not as a member of the Government, invested with such share of the executive power as only belongs to a responsible Minister of Finance, but as an adviser or a counsellor, whose suggestions or advice may or not be sanctioned by Your Majesty.[96]

The King approved Rolin Jacquemyn's proposal, although apparently there was opposition from some ministers,[97] and instructed the General Adviser to find a suitable man for the post. Rolin Jacquemyns immediately wrote to Lord Cromer in Egypt, for prior to his appointment in Siam, he had been in the Egyptian administration.[98] Lord Cromer suggested Alfred Mitchell-Innes, a 31 year-old British official who had been in Cairo since 1891.[99] There, in late 1895, the matter rested, for the British Foreign Office, which had to approve Mitchell-Innes' release, was unwilling to let the appointment proceed for fear that it would jeopardize Anglo-French negotiations over Siam, then in progress.[100] With the signing in January 1896 of an Anglo-French agreement to guarantee the independence of the Chao Phraya plain, the political obstacles on the British side to the appointment were removed. The following month King Chulalongkorn approved the engagement of Mitchell-Innes,[101] and the first financial adviser arrived in Bangkok in June 1896.[102]

The second major change at the Ministry of Finance took place in August 1896 when, as part of a general reordering of ministerial positions, Prince Sirithat was transferred to the Ministry of the Privy Seal, and Prince Mahit Rātchaharithai, who had been Minister of the Palace from 1887, became Minister of Finance. This was to be an important appointment, for Prince Mahit was to remain at the Ministry of Finance for almost ten years, giving it the continuity and drive which, until then, it had lacked.

Notes

1. David K. Wyatt, *The Politics of Reform in Thailand. Education in the Reign of King Chulalongkorn*, New Haven, 1969, pp. 85–7, 93 fn. 16.
2. *Rātchasakunwong* [Royal Genealogy], Bangkok, 1969.
3. Chao Phrayā Rattanabǫdin to Chulalongkorn, 1886, NA r5 Kh 14/3. In fact it appears that the *Kalāhōm* had been remitting its opium revenue to the Finance Office since 1884/5: Accounts of opium revenue for Bangkok and Provinces collected by the *Kalāhōm* and remitted to the Finance Office, 1884/5–1890/1, NA r5 Kh 14.1k/4.
4. Correspondence in NA r5 Kh 14/3.
5. Narāthip to Chulalongkorn, 11 February 1892, NA r5 Kh 1/5.
6. In 1892/3, the first year for which there are adequate figures, these farms (but including the lottery farm) contributed 7.5 million *baht* to the treasury, out of a total revenue of 15.3 million *baht*: *RFAB* 1903/4, p. 22.
7. Accounts of opium revenue for Bangkok and Provinces collected by the *Kalāhōm* and remitted to the Finance Office, 1884/5–1890/1, NA r5 Kh 14.1k/4.
8. G. William Skinner, *Chinese Society in Thailand: An Analytical History*, Ithaca, 1957, p. 121.
9. Ibid., p. 140
10. Joint letter from the committee to Chulalongkorn, 4 January 1890, NA r5 Kh 14.1k/1. Chao Phrayā Rattanabǫdin was the Minister of the *Mahātthai*.
11. 'Supplementary Law Relating to the Opium Monopoly', 1890, NA r5 Kh 2/1.
12. Notes on the 1890 opium monopoly auction: attached to Accounts of opium revenue for Bangkok and Provinces collected by the *Kalāhōm* and remitted to the Finance Office, 1884/5–1890/1, NA r5 Kh 14.1k/4. In 1890 the estimated total opium revenue, including the government's profit from the import and preparation of opium, was put at 2.68 million *baht*: in the mid-1880s the opium revenue had averaged 1.6 million *baht*.
13. Prince Damrong, *Ru'ang tamnān kānlōekbǭnbia lae lōek huai* [The Abolition of Gambling Dens and the Huai Lottery], Bangkok, 1960, pp. 37–45.
14. Ibid., pp. 37, 41–2. Narāthip to Chulalongkorn, 13 November 1891, NA r5 Kh 14.1kh/1[g]. The suffix [g] distinguishes this series of files from

those concerned with the spirit monopoly. In both cases, the series is denoted by 14.1kh: but the 'kh' is, in Thai, a different letter.

15. Unfortunately no figures are available for the Bangkok area alone or for the period prior to 1892. However, between 1892 and 1896, when no more dens were closed, the revenue from all the dens in the kingdom rose from 1.8 million *baht* to 2.9 million *baht*: *RFAB* 1903/4, p. 22.
16. An outline of the 1886 and 1887 laws can be constructed from scattered references in NA r5 Kh 14.1kh/1–39.
17. Instructions to provincial governors from Chulalongkorn, December 1889, NA r5 Kh 14.1kh/2.
18. Anuman Rajadhon, *Tamnān sunlakākǫn* [History of the Customs Department], Bangkok, 1939, pp. 96, 118. However, according to Anuman Rajadhon, the import duty on foreign spirits was attributed to the farmers until 1901. Apparently, between 1889 and 1901 the duty was collected by the Customs Department, passed to the appropriate farmer, who then made the payment to the treasury, together with the other payments due in connection with the farm.
19. The following figures are given by Wira Wimoniti, *Historical Patterns of Tax Administration in Thailand*, Bangkok, 1961, p. 114.

Treasury Revenue Receipts 1882–1889 (million baht)

1882: 6.92	1886: 13.66
1883: 7.39	1887: 12.09
1884: 6.03	1888: 13.65
1885: 6.08	1889: 12.02

The break between 1885 and 1886 is very dramatic. Yet figures of the same order of magnitude were quoted in Narāthip to Chulalongkorn, 17 March 1893, NA r5 Kh 3/1. 1886 was the year in which the *Kalāhōm* agreed to remit all its revenue receipts to the Finance Office.

20. 'Act Concerning the Functions of the Ministry of Finance', 7 October 1890, NA r5 Kh 1/5. The Act is quoted in full in Wichai Prasangsit, *Prawatsanphākǫn* [History of Taxation], Bangkok, 1971, pp. 305–13.
21. Ibid., clause 1.
22. Ibid., sections 4 and 5.
23. 'Privy Purse Department Act', 20 October 1890, NA r5 Kh 9.1/1.
24. *Prawat samnakngān phra khlang khāngthī* [History of the Privy Purse Department], Bangkok, 1967, pp. 13–15.
25. Presumably this applied only to the rent and interest earned on assets attributed to the Privy Purse. The King and the royal family had very considerable assets: it would appear unlikely that all those assets, and the income from them, came within the provisions of this legislation.
26. '*Krom Kep* Act', 13 December 1890, NA r5 Kh 2/2.
27. Narāthip to Chulalongkorn, 20 November 1890, NA r5 Kh 1/5.
28. Narāthip to Chulalongkorn, 11 December 1891, NA r5 Kh 1/5.
29. There exists in the National Archives no record of the discussions that took place to produce this budget, or indeed a copy of the budget itself. However, a detailed statement of government revenue and expenditure

for the period from 1892/3 was published in *RFAB* 1903/4, pp. 22–3: of course that is a statement of actual revenue and expenditure, not of the budget estimates.

30. Sir Henry Norman, 'Urgency in Siam', *Contemporary Review*, LXIV (1893), p. 738. For a consideration of the internal political circumstances of Siam in the early 1890s, see Wyatt, *The Politics of Reform in Thailand*, chap. 4.
31. Sir Henry Norman, *The Peoples and Politics of the Far East*, London, 1895, p. 451. It is important to note that for the period up to 1896–1897, the Siamese documentary evidence is rather scanty and disorganized, a reflection of the underdeveloped state of administrative procedures and then the virtual collapse of government. For this reason, for this period it is necessary to rely to a considerable extent on Norman's observations, although as Wyatt points out (op. cit., p. 95, fn. 18) some of his opinions are highly questionable. At the same time, the limited primary evidence does support his general picture.
32. W. A. Graham, *Siam: A Handbook of Practical, Commercial and Political Information*, London, 1924, vol. 1, p. 338
33. Wyatt, *The Politics of Reform in Thailand*, p. 96; Narāthip to Chulalongkorn, 26 April 1892, NA r5 Kh 1/9. Prince Narāthip was a leading literary figure.
34. Graham, op. cit., p. 338.
35. In a letter to the King on 28 January 1893 (NA r5 Kh 20.1/12), Prince Narāthip referred to 'imminent' legislation that would forbid government departments from maintaining accounts at the Bangkok banks.
36. Narāthip to Chulalongkorn, 30 July 1891, NA r5 Kh 1/5.
37. Chulalongkorn to Council of Ministers, 28 June 1892, NA r5 Kh 5.1/3.
38. Narāthip to Chulalongkorn, 1 November 1890, NA r5 Kh 11.1/1.
39. Narāthip to Phrayā Mahā Yōthā, 6 January 1893, NA r5 Kh 10.1/1; Narāthip to Chulalongkorn, 17 November 1891, NA r5 Kh 10/1; R. S. Le May, *The Coinage of Siam*, Bangkok, 1932, p. 85.
40. For example, the police forces of the capital were reorganized to ensure that all coolies working in Bangkok could be traced and taxed. In addition, new certificates of taxation and wrist seals were produced. Narāthip to Chulalongkorn, 5 June 1891, 15 July 1891, NA r5 Kh 13.1/1.
41. Report of Prince Devawongse's committee, 11 March 1893, NA r5 Kh 5.2/1.
42. Narāthip to Chulalongkorn, 11 December 1891, NA r5 Kh 1/5.
43. Narāthip to Chulalongkorn, 23 January 1892, NA r5 Kh 1/5.
44. Narāthip to Chulalongkorn, 31 March 1892, NA r5 Kh 1/5.
45. Narāthip to Chulalongkorn, 22 December 1892, NA r5 Kh 1/5.
46. It is difficult to provide accurate figures for the total number of officials employed in the Ministry in this early period. The Royal Gazette [*Rātchakitčhānubēksā*] periodically published lists of the officials in each ministry: but comparisons over time are difficult, partly because there were changing views as to which positions would be regarded as of sufficient importance to be included in the Gazette, and partly because a single official could hold several posts. However, the issue for 20 April

1890 (vol. 7, pp. 32–4) listed some 70 positions in the Finance Office: the issue for 5 June 1892 (vol. 9, pp. 62–5) listed 134 posts in the Ministry of Finance on 1 April 1892.

47. It is extremely difficult, perhaps impossible, to provide figures for this early period, for prior to 1892/3 the expenditures of individual ministries were not published. However, some indication of the expansion in the expenditure of the Ministry of Finance at the beginning of the 1890s can be gathered from the fact that in 1892/3 its accounted expenditure was 763 000 *baht* but that in the following year, under a new Minister, it was cut to 308 000 *baht*. The figure for 1892/3 was not reached again until 1897/8. *RFAB* 1903/4, pp. 24–5.
48. Correspondence in NA r5 Kh 5.1/4.
49. Report of Prince Devawongse's committee, 11 March 1893, NA r5 Kh 5.2/1.
50. Ibid.
51. Anuman Rajadhon, 'Phraprawat phraworawongthōe phra ong čhao phrōmphong athirāt' [Biography of Prince Phrōm], in *Tamnān sunlakākǭn* [History of the Customs Department], Bangkok, 1939, p. ii.
52. Report of Prince Devawongse's committee, 11 March 1893, NA r5 Kh 5.2/1.
53. Report of Prince Devawongse's committee, 17 March 1893, NA r5 Kh 5.2/2.
54. Report of Prince Devawongse's committee, 11 March 1893, NA r5 Kh 5.2/1.
55. Chulalongkorn to Sommot, 21 March 1893, NA r5 Kh 3/1.
56. Devawongse to Chulalongkorn, 20 March 1893, NA r5 Kh 3/1.
57. Narāthip to Chulalongkorn, 17 March 1893, NA r5 Kh 3/1.
58. Devawongse to Browne [Hongkong and Shanghai Bank], 20 March 1893, NA r5 Kh 3/1.
59. Devawongse to Chulalongkorn, 20 March 1893, NA r5 Kh 3/1.
60. Narāthip to Chulalongkorn, 17 March 1893, 19 March 1893, NA r5 Kh 3/1.
61. Chulalongkorn to Narāthip, 21 March 1893, NA r5 Kh 3/1.
62. *Rātchasakunwong* [Royal Genealogy], Bangkok, 1969. For a further comment on the resignation of Prince Narāthip see Suphāphǭn Čharanphat, 'Phrayā Suriyānuwat nai kitčhakānfin khǭng rathabān' [Phrayā Suriyānuwat and Government Administration of the Opium Monopoly], in Sirilak Sakkriangkrai (ed.), *Phrayā Suriyānuwat (Koet Bunnāk) naksētthasāt khonrāek khǭng mu'ang thai* [Phrayā Suriyānuwat (Koet Bunnāk): Thailand's First Economist], Bangkok, 1980, pp. 170–1.
63. David K. Wyatt, *The Politics of Reform in Thailand*, New Haven, 1969, p. 296.
64. D. G. E. Hall, *A History of South-East Asia*, London, 1968, pp. 679–701.
65. In November 1893 the British Minister in Bangkok informed the Foreign Office in London that over the preceding four months the King had lost three stones in weight and had abandoned all interest in life: Scott to Rosebery, 24 November 1893, PRO FO 69/150. In

June 1894 he reported that the King, now at Kǫ Si Chang, had a high fever and that it was believed that death was imminent: Scott to Kimberley, 21 June 1894, PRO FO 69/153. There is also some evidence on this subject from Robert Morant, the tutor to the Crown Prince, who was dismissed from his post in early 1894. On his return to London he wrote a 'Memorandum on the Present Political Situation in Siam. The Misleading Nature of the Current Reports thereon and the Grave Condition of her Internal Affairs', July 1894, which he submitted to the Foreign Office: PRO FO 17/1223. [This document appears in Nigel Brailey, *Two Views of Siam on the Eve of the Chakri Reformation*, Whiting Bay, Arran, 1989, pp. 85–105] Because of the circumstances surrounding his departure from Siam, Morant certainly cannot be regarded as an independent observer (and in this context it is important to note that he was Sir Henry Norman's principal informant) but presumably he was one of the very few foreigners to see the King regularly at this time. Morant wrote that in August 1893 the King 'was as nearly as possible imbecile...though it is at the same time incorrect to suppose that he is or has been in a condition of pronounced active insanity'. Although he had since improved, Morant suggested that 'he has lost all will-power and all initiative, is a prey to perpetual despondency, and also entirely "possessed" by the spirit of distrust and suspicion of *everyone* who approaches him'. See also Wyatt, op. cit., pp. 95–6; Sir Henry Norman, *The Peoples and Politics of the Far East,* London, 1895, pp. 435–9, 451–3.

66. Norman, op. cit., pp. 451–2.
67. Chulalongkorn to Narit, 27 February 1894, NA r5 Kh 5.1/4.
68. The Ministry of the Palace complained to the King that it had received little funds from the treasury: Official in the Ministry of the Palace to Chulalongkorn, 26 November 1894, NA r5 Kh 5.1/4.
69. W. A. Graham, *Siam*, London, 1924, vol. 1, p. 338. This situation was well reflected in the statements of accounted expenditure. Total expenditure fell from 18.17 million *baht* in 1893/4 to 12.48 million *baht* in 1894/5. More significantly, the accounted expenditure of the Ministry of the Interior was, at 205 000 *baht*, the lowest of all the ministries in 1894/5 except the Ministry of Justice: *RFAB* 1903/4, p. 24. It is evident that to a very considerable extent, the Ministry of the Interior was financing itself outside the budget – from its own sources of revenue.
70. Narāthip to Mǫm Čhao Sawāt [Director of the *Krom Sanphākǭn*], 20 March 1893, NA r5 Kh 14.1k/10.
71. Phra Phakdīphatarākǭn to Chulalongkorn, undated, NA r5 Kh 14.1k/11.
72. Narāthip to Sommǫt, 21 March 1893, NA r5 Kh 14.1k/10.
73. Narāthip to Mǫm Čhao Sawāt, 20 March 1893, NA r5 Kh 14.1k/10.
74. Sommot to Chulalongkorn, 5 November 1893, NA r5 Kh 9.1/1, enclosing amendments to the 1890 Privy Purse Department Act; *Prawat samnakngān phra khlang khāngthī* [History of the Privy Purse Department], Bangkok, 1967, p. 17.
75. Report of Prince Devawongse's committee, 11 March 1893, NA r5 Kh 5.2/1.

76. Narit to Chulalongkorn, 23 January 1894, NA r5 Kh 14.2/2.
77. Narit to Chulalongkorn, 4 June 1894, NA r5 Kh 13.1/5; accounts in NA r5 Kh 13.1/5.
78. Total government revenue, in *baht* millions, was: 1892/3, 15.37; 1893/4, 17.38; 1894/5, 17.33: *RFAB* 1903/4, p. 22.
79. de Bunsen to Bertie, 16 December 1894, PRO FO 69/153.
80. In September 1894 Rolin Jacquemyns, the General Adviser, wrote to the King outlining a series of urgently needed administrative and judicial reforms. His suggestions met with the King's general approval: Scott to Kimberley, 20 October 1894, and enclosures, PRO FO 69/153.
81. 'Phraprawat somdet čhaofā kromphrayā naritsarānuwattiwong' [Biography of Prince Narit], in *Banthu'k ru'ang khwāmrū tāngtāng* [Notes on Various Knowledge]: correspondence between Prince Narit and Phrayā Anuman Rajadhon: Bangkok, 1963, vol. 2, p. 21.
82. Phra Phakdīphatarākǭn to Chulalongkorn, May 1894, NA r5 Kh 14.1k/11.
83. Sirithat to Chulalongkorn, 17 May 1895; Chulalongkorn to Sirithat, 18 May 1895, NA r5 Kh 14.1k/11.
84. Anuman Rajadhon, 'Phraprawat phraworawongthōe phra ong čhao phrōmphong athirāt' [Biography of Prince Phrōm], in *Tamnān sunlakākǭn* [History of the Customs Department], Bangkok, 1939, pp. iv–viii.
85. Sirithat to Chulalongkorn, 15 March 1895, NA r5 Kh 5.1/4.
86. Council of Ministers to Chulalongkorn, 6 October 1895, NA r5 Kh 5.1/4.
87. Chulalongkorn to Sirithat, 15 October 1895, NA r5 Kh 5.1/4.
88. Sirithat to Sommot, 24 January 1896, NA r5 Kh 5.1/5.
89. Ibid.
90. Sirithat to Chulalongkorn, 3 March 1896, NA r5 Kh 5.1/5.
91. Chulalongkorn to Sirithat, 22 April 1896, NA r5 Kh 5.1/2.
92. List attached to: Mahit to Chulalongkorn, 23 September 1896, NA r5 Kh 5.1/5.
93. The ideas in this paragraph are taken from an unsigned, undated memorandum found in the file concerned with the 1896/7 budget: NA r5 Kh 5.1/5. The author was almost certainly either Prince Sirithat or his successor, Prince Mahit.
94. Narāthip to Chulalongkorn, 24 April 1890, NA r5 Kh 1/5.
95. Rolin Jacquemyns to Chulalongkorn, 15 February 1896: enclosed in de Bunsen to Salisbury, 20 February 1896, PRO FO 69/169.
96. Ibid.
97. de Bunsen to Salisbury, 28 February 1896, PRO FO 628, Box 18, No. 242.
98. Christian de Saint-Hubert, 'Rolin Jacquemyns (Chao Phya Aphay Raja) and the Belgian Legal Advisers in Siam at the turn of the Century', *Journal of the Siam Society*, 53, 2 (July 1965), pp. 181–90.
99. *Foreign Office List*, 1951.
100. Cromer to de Bunsen, 31 December 1895, PRO FO 633, Cromer Papers, vol. 8.

101. Chulalongkorn to Rolin Jacquemyns, 16 February 1896: enclosed in de Bunsen to Salisbury, 18 February 1896, PRO FO 69/169.
102. Sirithat to Chulalongkorn, 15 August 1896, NA r5 Kh 1/16.

3 The Creation of an Effective Ministry of Finance, 1896–1902

Prince Mahit's term as Minister of Finance was so long and formed such an important period in the early history of the Ministry that it will be considered over two chapters, the first covering the period from August 1896 until the middle of 1902, the second from mid-1902 until the resignation of Prince Mahit in mid-1906. The first period was dominated by Prince Mahit's attempts to establish the Ministry of Finance as an effective and influential component within the government. And in the period from mid-1902 the Ministry was concerned with major financial initiatives, notably exchange reform and the raising of the first sterling loan in Europe, and with the prospect of substantial budget deficits.

3.1 THE ESTABLISHMENT OF BUDGETARY CONTROL

On his appointment as Minister of Finance in 1896, Prince Mahit took as his immediate and most important task the need to establish effective budgetary procedures for controlling the administration's expenditures. The new Minister inherited from Prince Sirithat the incomplete estimates for the year then in progress, 1896/7.[1] A rapidly completed budget was sanctioned by the King on 13 October 1896.[2] The following financial year, 1897/8, gave Prince Mahit his first real opportunity to improve the effectiveness of the Ministry's budget procedures. In fact there was very considerable pressure on the Ministry of Finance to complete that budget on time (by the beginning of April 1897), for in that month King Chulalongkorn was to leave Bangkok for his first visit to Europe, and Prince Mahit was to be in the royal party. In late 1896 the Ministry of Finance despatched its standard request to each ministry and department that they submit their preliminary estimates to it by 15 December, and it would appear that the majority of ministries complied.[3] In January 1897 Prince Mahit followed this up with a letter to each government department asking that in future they submit detailed statements of current expenditure together with the preliminary estimates for the coming year.[4] Prince Mahit explained that it was important that the Ministry of Finance have accurate information on the current expenditure of a department when it came to assess its future expenditure demands: it was particularly important that the Ministry should have clear evidence that a department had spent its allocation in the current year before it considered an increased estimate for the following one. Two months later Prince Mahit despatched officials from the *Kǫng Sārabānchī* to each government department to instruct the officials there in the accounts and audit methods which the Ministry of Finance wished to establish throughout the administration.[5] With uniform procedures in place, the Ministry of Finance would be able to establish speedily and accurately the financial position of each ministry and department.

In February 1897 the King lent his weight in support of Prince Mahit's measures when, in a letter to the Minister, a letter which was to be circulated in the Council, he strongly stated the responsibilities and functions of the Minister of Finance.[6] It was by far the most forceful statement of his position since the establishment of the Ministry of Finance in 1890.

1. The Minister of Finance has full authority and full responsibility in all matters directly or indirectly concerning the Ministry of Finance.
2. The Minister of Finance has the authority to issue regulations and instructions to other ministries on matters concerning the Ministry of Finance: all ministries must obey those instructions and regulations.
3. When the Minister of Finance thinks it necessary to investigate any financial matter in another ministry or in the

provinces, a matter which concerns the Ministry of Finance, then he has the authority to make that investigation – to call for accounts and records – without obstruction.

4. With regard to all the officials who are involved in the compiling of accounts, right down to the clerks who receive the accounts, the Ministry of Finance has the responsibility to examine their knowledge and their methods, and of deciding whether they are adequate for their posts or not.[7]

There seems little doubt that the King's statement referred principally to the responsibility of the Ministry of Finance in the compilation of the budget.

Prince Mahit's measures and the King's intervention had a considerable effect. On 20 March 1897 Prince Mahit could report to the King that the Ministry of Finance was ready to present the completed estimates to the Council of Ministers.[8] The budget discussions took place throughout late March and early April. Proposed expenditure considerably exceeded estimated revenue. But partly because the King quickly agreed to a reduction in the expenditure allocation of the Privy Purse Department,[9] thereby setting an example which undoubtedly he expected to be followed, and partly because Prince Mahit submitted to the Council a list of expenditure initiatives that might be postponed, reduced or abandoned altogether, agreement appears to have been reached quite rapidly.[10] The budget for 1897/8 was sanctioned by the King on 6 April,[11] and the following day the royal party left Bangkok for Europe.[12]

In the absence of Prince Mahit, Prince Narit became acting Minister of Finance, while continuing as Minister of War. Prince Narit, a notably unenergetic Minister in his own right in 1893–1894, was if anything even more inactive in 1897. Very few documents exist from the Ministry of Finance in the period of Prince Mahit's absence: and those few indicate that Prince Narit's main concern was to defer all decisions, no matter how small, until the King returned from Europe.

Immediately on the arrival of the royal party back in Bangkok (on 16 December 1897),[13] Prince Mahit was again deeply involved in work on the budget. He was angered to find that, despite the success of the previous year in having the budget completed on time and despite the fact that at the beginning of November each ministry and province had been reminded to submit preliminary estimates to the Ministry of Finance by 15 December,[14] a large number of estimates were still outstanding. By the middle of January 1898 no estimates had been received from the Ministries of Public Works, Public Instruction, the Capital, the Palace and War; or from 13 provinces. A warning letter was sent to each offender by the King.[15] Only the Ministry of War and five provinces responded immediately. Following a further complaint from Prince Mahit, on 2 February the King wrote again to each of the errant ministers and officials – including Prince Damrong, who was responsible for the expenditure estimates of the provinces – to point out that it needed only one ministry to overstep the deadlines demanded by the Ministry of Finance for the whole of the government's budget process to be seriously disrupted.[16]

By 15 March all the preliminary expenditure estimates had been examined by the Ministry of Finance, and the Minister was ready to submit the budget to the Council of Ministers. But Prince Mahit, as he confessed to the King, faced the budget discussions with little enthusiasm.[17] It was not simply that he was disturbed by the apparent need to cajole his colleagues repeatedly if they were to submit their preliminary estimates on schedule. Prince Mahit's concern went deeper. He was disturbed by the spirit in which his colleagues compiled their expenditure requests, and consequently by the criteria which were applied when those estimates were examined by the Ministry of Finance and then approved by the Council of Ministers. Prince Mahit argued that the Council approached discussion of the budget with no agreement as to the basic priorities for government expenditure. As a result the discussions (if that was the word) often degenerated into drawn-out disputes over relatively unimportant items of expenditure.

The Minister brought further of his fears to the attention of the King in a second letter, on 19 March 1898.[18] According to his calculations, the estimated revenue for 1898/9 was 26 million *baht*. The total of the preliminary expenditure allocations sought by the ministries came to 29.45 million *baht*: therefore 3.45 million *baht* had to be cut from the ministries' expenditure demands if a budget deficit was to be avoided. The problem had two aspects. In a situation where the government's total expenditure was rising rapidly as a result of the marked expansion in the administration's functions and responsibilities, it was extremely difficult for the Ministry of Finance, in the time available to it, to identify those expenditure demands which were unjustified or extravagant. Yet, Prince Mahit continued, an examination of the actual expenditures of individual ministries over the past few years, compared with their expenditure estimates for those years, showed that commonly they requested and obtained expenditure allocations considerably in excess of the sums that they could use. At the end of each year they were left with substantial unspent funds. In short, the projected budget deficit for 1898/9 was almost certainly more apparent than real. The Ministry of Finance, therefore, had to ensure that the ministries submitted expenditure requests which accurately reflected their spending capacity rather than embraced impractical notions of what they might wish to spend.

Prince Mahit argued that inflated salary estimates caused the Ministry of Finance by far the most serious difficulties. There were no regulations to govern the number of officials in each government department; there were no salary scales. When it came to examine the ministries' preliminary expenditure estimates, the Ministry of Finance was faced with innumerable demands for increases in salaries and positions. To examine each in detail was impossible. As a result, they were rejected or approved in an almost random manner. Inevitably, Prince Mahit admitted, some unjustified demands had been passed, some well-justified demands had been refused. But the solution was clear: to establish a standard structure in which all officials were paid the same salary for the same responsibilities, and in which the same number of officials would be appointed to carry out the same volume and class of work in all departments across the administration. With this structure in place, the appointment of officials and increases in salaries would be removed from the preliminary examination of the estimates undertaken by the Ministry of Finance and from the budget discussions undertaken by the Council of Ministers. The Ministry and the Council would be able to give their time to the important expenditure proposals. Prince Mahit therefore recommended the establishment of a committee to determine, in consultation with the appropriate ministers and heads of department, the responsibilities of each part of the administration, the number of officials required to carry out those responsibilities, and the salaries they were to receive.

The Minister of Finance concluded his letter to the King with a few further suggestions: that expenditure sanctioned under one head could not be transferred simply on the initiative of the ministry concerned to another head; that the ministries would not be allowed to maintain their own reserve funds to meet unexpected demands for expenditure but rather that all reserves would be held in a single account controlled by the Ministry of Finance.[19]

Prince Mahit's letter was read to the Council of Ministers on 26 March 1898.[20] The ministers were in basic agreement with his recommendations, although some reservations were expressed, notably by Prince Damrong. The Minister of the Interior appears to have been concerned, in particular, that Prince Mahit's proposals might give too much authority to the Ministry of Finance. In holding down government expenditure, he argued, 'we must not get into the position where a head of department would be able to say – because the Ministry of Finance is unlikely to allow me the necessary funds, therefore I am unable to carry out my projects'.[21] Prince Damrong's unease at the prospect of a strong Ministry of Finance was here openly stated.

Prince Mahit met each reservation and criticism. He then sought to impress on the Council the central objective of his proposals:

> My real wish is this: to have the budget discussions completed speedily, to have new major items of expenditure discussed, as to whether we should proceed with them or not, whether we can afford to proceed with them or not. For the fact is that we are faced with a situation of rapidly increasing expenditure which cannot all be covered by revenue. Therefore there has to be discussion and decision as to the order of priorities for expenditure.[22]

The Council of Ministers gave general approval to Prince Mahit's proposals. The King then followed up these discussions by asking the Financial Adviser, Mitchell-Innes, for his views on the processes by which the government produced its budget.[23] The latter had a number of practical suggestions, to complement the Minister's earlier proposals.[24] While these further discussions were taking place, the Ministry of Finance and the Council of Ministers were engaged on the final stages of preparing the budget for 1898/9. The completed estimates were sent to the King on 20 April 1898,[25] and the budget was sanctioned three days later.[26]

In the long struggle of the Ministry of Finance to create and maintain effective procedures for the allocation of the government's expenditures, the period from December 1898 until June 1899, which saw the completion of the budget for 1899/1900, was to prove crucial. At the beginning of this period, the Ministry of Finance was faced again with the inability, or perhaps, in view of the apparent uneasiness within the government over Prince Mahit's increasingly forceful stand, the unwillingness of the ministries to submit their preliminary expenditure estimates to it on time. On 31 December 1898, 15 days after the deadline for the submission of estimates, the Ministry of Finance had received nothing from the Ministries of the Palace, Foreign Affairs, the Interior, the Capital and Public Works, or from 10 provinces.[27] The King felt that the time had come to deliver his most severe rebuke. In a long letter to each minister, he pointed out that the raising and spending of the kingdom's revenues was no longer a matter which affected the throne alone: it now affected every Siamese.[28] As the responsibilities of the government were now much greater than they had been in the past, the failure to allocate sufficient funds to a ministry, or the failure to allocate funds wisely, could severely damage the effectiveness of the administration. Ultimately it could threaten the stability and independence of the kingdom. The King continued:

> I do not want you to regard, to consider without thinking, these strict budget regulations as simply a ceremony or simply an import from the west. It is true that they come from the west, but we are using them because they will bring stability and certainty [to the government's finances]. Do not think that we are merely adopting the outer forms of such procedures, just so that we can give the impression that all [our finances] are in order, that all is beautiful. These regulations must really be applied.[29]

The King made it clear that never again did he wish to hear that the ministries were late in submitting their expenditure estimates, and to emphasize the point he instructed each minister to inform him directly, immediately they presented their estimates to the Ministry of Finance. The ministries responded quickly to the King's reproaches, and by mid–January 1899 the Ministry of Finance had received sufficient preliminary estimates to begin the final work on the budget.[30]

In this task the Ministry was assisted for the first time by a European Controller-General, Charles James Rivett-Carnac, who had arrived in Bangkok in early December 1898.[31] In examining the preliminary estimates, Rivett-Carnac was struck, as Prince Mahit had been the previous year, by the large number of requests for lavish increases in salaries and official positions, requests which, he argued, the Ministry of Finance was unable to consider in detail but which, if sanctioned, would soon bankrupt the treasury.[32] To meet this problem Rivett-Carnac took up his Minister's earlier proposal for the establishment of a committee to determine the salary and functions of officials across the administration. In January 1899 the King gave his approval,[33] and the committee began work the following month.

The Committee on Establishments, as it was called, had three permanent members: Prince Narit (now Minister of Public Works), Mọm Čhao Alangkān (a senior official from the Ministry of Finance) and Rivett-Carnac. During the period in which a ministry was being investigated, that minister was appointed an *ex officio* member. It was decided to look first at the Ministry of Justice.[34] The committee met on six occasions in February and March 1899, and its investigation involved it in visits not only to the Ministry of Justice itself but also to the courts and prisons under its authority. The Minister of Justice had requested salaries for 552 officials in the estimate for 1899/1900. The committee reduced that figure to 469: and the Minister's estimates for salaries was reduced from 645 240 *baht* to 628 824 *baht*.[35] The committee did not, therefore, secure a substantial reduction in the salary estimates. But that was not its aim. As Rivett-Carnac argued, the object was to bring effective control to the increase of salaries and positions where none had existed before, to 'in future prevent the indiscriminate raising of a man's pay without proportionate increase in his work and responsibility'.[36] The committee achieved another objective. For the first time, this major element within the administration's routine expenditure estimates was removed from the direct responsibility of the Ministry of Finance and from the budget discussions of the Council of Ministers.

Unfortunately, after a promising, energetic beginning to its labours, the Committee on Establishments soon lost momentum, mainly because Prince Narit and Mọm Čhao Alangkān were frequently absent on other business. By June 1899 the work of the committee was at a standstill.[37] Only after Rivett-Carnac had sought an audience with the King did the committee resume its meetings, but even then, on the insistence of Prince Narit, it met only once a week.[38] Four meetings in June and July 1899 saw the committee complete its investigation of the Ministry of Foreign Affairs.[39] The investigation of the next ministry, the Ministry of the Interior, was perfunctory. It concerned only the offices in

Bangkok and not the provincial administration, it was attended not by Prince Damrong but by his deputy, and it lasted only ninety-five minutes.[40] The superficiality of the examination of one of the most important ministries is very strange and, with the evidence available, inexplicable. Finally, over the period September to December 1899 the committee held four meetings to investigate the Ministry of Finance itself. The number of officials allowed for in the estimates was reduced from 864 to 862, although there was a substantial reallocation of positions within the Ministry; the salary estimate was increased from 562 188 *baht* to 581 028 *baht*.[41] There the investigations by the committee came to a halt until 1901. From December 1899 through to the following March the committee prepared its reports on the Ministries of Justice, Foreign Affairs, the Interior and Finance, and submitted them to Prince Mahit, who then placed them before the King.

At about the time the Committee on Establishments had started its work, Prince Mahit had begun his examination of the remaining preliminary expenditure estimates for 1899/1900. The Minister found this a considerable strain. In either February or March 1899 he wrote a long letter to King Chulalongkorn, outlining the problems faced by the Ministry of Finance in compiling accurate and realistic expenditure budgets, and complaining of the apparent inability of his ministerial colleagues to co-operate fully in the presentation and revision of their expenditure demands.[42] He noted that the King had had to intervene forcefully in order to ensure that the ministries submitted their estimates on schedule; the King's intervention implied a failure on the part of the Ministry of Finance. In fact this letter, like many which Prince Mahit wrote to the King in this period, had two, almost contradictory, moods. On the one hand there was despair and dejection, protestations by the Minister of his unworthiness for the position he held. Not for the first or the last time, Prince Mahit stated his willingness, almost eagerness, to leave the Ministry of Finance if the King could find a replacement. There is no reason to doubt the Minister's sincerity here. Yet on the other hand, in the same letter, there was an equally unmistakable determination to establish and maintain effective budget procedures – to see the task through. There is no evidence that Prince Mahit's departure was seriously contemplated by Chulalongkorn at this time.

The total expenditure requests for 1899/1900 came to 38.5 million *baht*, but the Ministry of Finance was able to cut this immediately to 33.48 million *baht*. The estimated revenue for 1899/1900 was 30.42 million *baht*.[43] Rivett-Carnac argued that although the treasury reserves could easily cover the projected deficit of 3.06 million *baht*, the Ministry of Finance should still impose further cuts in expenditure to produce a budget surplus.[44] His principal argument was that sooner or later Siam would have to raise a loan in Europe to continue construction of the kingdom's railway network, and that in order to facilitate this the government would need to publish its annual budget and a statement of its financial position. If the budget showed a deficit, for whatever reason, European investors would be reluctant to take up the loan on any but the most stringent terms.

Rivett-Carnac stated where the cuts might be made: principally a cut of 2.57 million *baht* from the army and navy estimates, and a reduction of 1 million *baht* in the allocation for railway construction (in anticipation that construction would soon be financed by means of a European loan). In addition a small immediate saving was to be secured as a result of the King's decision to accept in future a fixed allocation of 6 million *baht* for the Privy Purse and the Ministry of the Palace, instead of the 15 per cent of total government revenue as had been the case since 1890. According to Rivett-Carnac, these reductions would give a total expenditure estimate of 29.52 million *baht*, and a small budget surplus of 890 000 *baht*. Prince Mahit accepted the cuts proposed by Rivett-Carnac, although he recognized that some ministers could well object.[45] When the estimates were discussed by the Council of Ministers in late April and early May 1899, some small amendments were made, to bring total expenditure up to 30.11 million *baht*.[46] The budget was sanctioned by the King on 5 June.[47]

The Ministry of Finance completed its work on the 1899/1900

budget in a reasonably optimistic mood. In the first place, Rivett-Carnac, now Financial Adviser, in a memorandum which in form foreshadowed the *Report of the Financial Adviser on the Budget* which was to be published from 1901/2, drew an encouraging picture of the kingdom's financial position.[48] The government had very substantial cash reserves, more than 23.6 million *baht* in Bangkok and Singapore alone. This was a considerable achievement, for at the same time as the government had been building up these reserves, government expenditure itself had increased at a rapid rate.[49] Rivett-Carnac pointed out that over the period from 1891/2 to 1898/9 the government had spent 14.41 million *baht* on railway construction alone, entirely out of current revenue.

But in mid-1899 there were other encouraging signs for the Ministry. The Committee on Establishments had at last begun work although, as noted above, it was soon to lose its early momentum. More importantly there were indications that the Ministry of Finance was close to achieving its major objective – the establishment of efficient and effective budget procedures. The King's outburst in January 1899 had, it was hoped, at last convinced the ministers that it was important that they submit their preliminary expenditure estimates to the Ministry of Finance on schedule. In addition, despite Prince Mahit's pessimism, it would appear that the ministries were now co-operating more freely with the Ministry of Finance in amending and revising their estimates, and that the Council of Ministers in its budget discussions was concerning itself much more with the major items of expenditure. Certainly there were no longer any serious complaints from Prince Mahit to the King over lack of co-operation from his colleagues. There may also have been some numerical evidence to indicate improvement. Whereas in 1898/9 the ministries had been unable to spend 5 million *baht* of the funds allocated to them, in 1899/1900 this was reduced to 3 million *baht*[50] – which may suggest that the administration could now produce more accurate and realistic expenditure allocations.

There was a further important aspect of the Ministry's attempts to improve the efficiency of its budget procedures – the development of a more effective and comprehensive system of audit and account. There was little benefit to be gained if the Ministry of Finance, having persuaded the ministries to co-operate in compiling accurate and realistic expenditure estimates, were then to impose no check on actual expenditure. As Rivett-Carnac had been engaged as Controller-General (although within two months of his arrival in Siam in December 1898 he had been appointed Financial Adviser) it was one of his major responsibilities to reform the administration's audit and account procedures. From 1899 the Ministry of Finance produced scores of regulations to cover every possible financial transaction within the administration.[51] In the majority of cases the regulations were based on regulations then in use in the British India administration. In the absence of documentary evidence it is impossible to assess the effectiveness of these new regulations, although Rivett-Carnac was occasionally pleased to refer to improvements in the government's audit and accounting methods.[52] The fact that from the late 1890s the ministries were spending a higher proportion of their expenditure allocations may have reflected a realization on their part that they would later be subject to a detailed audit by the Ministry of Finance.

The budget for the following year, 1900/1, was prepared without serious complications. Indeed the Ministry of Finance found time for a more detailed examination of the estimates than had ever before been possible,[53] and still had the budget sanctioned by the King by 1 April.[54] It was the first time that the budget had been completed for the beginning of the Siamese year. The improvement was maintained in 1901/2. For the first time, Prince Mahit's budget memoranda and correspondence were mainly concerned with the actual revision and amendment of the expenditure proposals submitted to the Ministry of Finance. In contrast to the position in the immediately preceding years, little attention had to be given to the budget procedures as such.[55]

Perhaps the most significant feature of the budget discussions which took place in March 1901 was that there were few serious disputes between the Ministry of Finance and the other ministries over the revision and amendment of the preliminary expenditure estimates, despite the fact that in order to secure a budget surplus, cuts totalling 13 million *baht* had to be made.[56] The near absence of serious disagreement might be explained by a number of considerations.[57] Although the Ministry of Finance proposed large cuts in some estimates – a request from the Ministry of Public Works for 5.24 million *baht* for railway construction was reduced to 2 million *baht* – both Prince Mahit and Rivett-Carnac demonstrated a clear willingness to discuss thoroughly any expenditure proposal with the relevant ministry; and they were quite prepared to change their mind as a result of broader discussion. Second, Prince Mahit and Rivett-Carnac refused to discuss requests for increases in salaries or increases in staff but referred them to the Committee on Establishments. It was therefore significant that that committee took up its investigations again in February 1901. The General Adviser's Department was examined on 28 February,[58] the Ministry of Public Works in the following month,[59] the navy in September 1901,[60] and the army in December.[61] But in 1902 the committee once again came to a standstill, through the frequent absences of the chairman, Prince Narit.[62] In December 1902, after Rivett-Carnac had threatened to resign from the committee unless Prince Narit was replaced,[63] Prince Čhanthaburī, the Controller-General, was appointed chairman.[64] The Committee on Establishments limped on for several years, finally concluding its work in January 1905 with an investigation of the Ministry of War.[65] The third possible reason why few serious disputes arose during the discussions of the 1901/2 budget is that the Ministry of Finance cut many of its own preliminary estimates: there were to be no grounds for the accusation that the Ministry was using its position to protect its own expenditure. The 1901/2 budget was submitted to the King on 19 April 1901,[66] and was sanctioned on 27 April.[67]

In compiling this budget the Ministry of Finance had attempted, as was its practice, to secure a small revenue surplus. But its calculations were upset at the last moment by news that the international arbitrator appointed to settle a dispute between the

Siamese government and the original contractor for the construction of the Bangkok–Korat railway, Murray Campbell, had decided in favour of the latter and awarded compensation of £161 000, or 2.8 million *baht*.[68] As a result, for the first time the budget provided for a revenue deficit, of 2.5 million *baht*, to be covered from the treasury reserve. A projected deficit at this point was particularly unfortunate as the administration had decided to publish the budget estimates, together with a report by the Financial Adviser. As one of the major aims of publication was to bring Siam's recent financial and administrative progress to the attention of Europe, as a prelude to the raising of a European loan, the deficit was an unhappy intrusion.

Rivett-Carnac presented his report to Prince Mahit on 18 April 1901.[69] Its content calls for little comment, as the Financial Adviser largely restricted himself to a detailed, rather dry description and analysis of the principal heads of revenue and expenditure. As might have been expected, Rivett-Carnac's conclusion was suitably glowing:

> the Government is in a remarkably strong financial position. The Revenues are showing themselves to be elastic and they are being rapidly got under better control. The Expenditure, also, is being more and more devoted to improvements in the Administration of the Government with a view to the safety, convenience, and happiness of the people, while the audit and control of the disbursements by the Financial Department is becoming real and effective.[70]

The *Report of the Financial Adviser on the Budget* was primarily an exercise in public relations, directed towards the Europeans, both in Bangkok and in Europe itself. Copies of the report were sent to the foreign representatives in Bangkok, to all the Siamese missions abroad,[71] and to Dr. Morrison, the Far East correspondent of *The Times*.[72] In September 1901 *The Times* published a long, and largely favourable, report on Siam's recent progress.[73]

There is little need to consider in detail the preparation of the budget for 1902/3, for the relative ease with which the estimates were compiled merely confirms the comparative stability and effectiveness of the budget procedures now attained. Similarly Rivett-Carnac's second budget report projected an air of confidence in the effectiveness of the administration's financial control, to contrast strongly with the fragility even of the late 1890s. But if the actual preparation of the 1902/3 budget calls for little comment, its content did raise important issues. In compiling the budget the Ministry of Finance found it difficult to reduce the expenditure estimates to secure a revenue surplus.[74] Indeed it was found necessary to meet a 3.5 million *baht* allocation for railway construction in part by drawing 1.5 million *baht* from the treasury reserves.[75] Thus, for the first time, the Ministry of Finance used the reserves to avoid a budget deficit.[76] This was the first clear indication of what would prove to be the Ministry's major budget problem in the 1900s: with the rate of increase in government revenue slowing down, yet legitimate requests for larger expenditure allocations increasing at an unprecedented pace, the administration would face tough decisions over its priorities.

3.2 THE MINISTRY OF FINANCE AND REVENUE COLLECTION

In its work on the budget between 1896 and 1902, the Ministry of Finance concerned itself almost exclusively with the expenditure side of the administration's finances. Revenue considerations were not, of course, ignored. Prince Mahit certainly had his share of difficulties with the major revenue farms, principally the spirit monopoly.[77] In addition, as was noted earlier, a host of regulations was issued in this period, concerned to tighten control over the flow of revenues into the treasury. Yet it is significant that in all his budget correspondence with the King between 1896 and 1902, Prince Mahit invariably took the figures for estimated revenues as given, and focused on the expenditure estimates. Such apparent prejudice ran counter to the provisions of the 1890 legislation which had established the Ministry of Finance;[78] yet it must be seen in the context of Prince Mahit's ambition, actually to divest the Ministry of responsibility for the collection of the government's revenue.

That policy was developed in a number of stages. First, in 1896, a distinction was introduced between financial administration and fiscal administration in the provinces – or at least in those parts of the kingdom where the *thēsāphibān* structure of local administration was in place.[79] In the early 1890s it was perhaps inevitable that as Prince Damrong had pushed ahead with the reform of provincial administration, the weak Ministry of Finance had been unable to exert much influence in the provinces. It was therefore the practice for the superintendent commissioners [*khāluang thēsāphibān*] to spend revenues first and then request the approval of the Ministry of Finance. In 1896 the provincial financial commissioners [*khāluang khlang*] were removed from the Ministry of the Interior and placed under the Ministry of Finance: the *khāluang thēsāphibān* now had to go to the *khāluang khlang*, representatives of the Ministry of Finance, for the funds for salaries and construction projects. However, responsibility for fiscal administration in the provinces was left with the superintendent commissioners.

The second stage in the development of this policy occurred in July 1898 when W. A. Graham, an adviser in the accounts department of the Ministry of the Capital,[80] wrote to Prince Mahit on the collection of taxes in Bangkok Province.[81] Graham pointed out that the Ministry of the Capital had recently taken over the collection of a number of taxes in the province, and that it was anticipated that before long all revenues raised there would be its responsibility, with the exception of the revenues from the major tax farms which would remain with the Ministry of Finance. Graham therefore proposed that a revenue office be established within the Ministry of the Capital; he ventured to suggest that he be made head of it. Graham's proposal was welcomed by the King and Prince Mahit.[82] The *Krom Sanphākǫn Nai*, the Bangkok Revenue Department, began work on 1 November 1898.

The establishment of the Bangkok Revenue Department, which was concerned primarily with the collection of land taxes, inevitably brought pressure for the creation of a comparable department for the provinces. By 1899 the collection of land taxes in the provinces outside the capital was causing some confusion. The decision made in 1896 to confirm the responsibility of the Ministry of the Interior for fiscal administration in the provinces was undermined by the fact that the collection of land taxes there (or at least the most important of those taxes, the *khānā*)[83] was in fact under the Ministry of Finance, for in 1897 that Ministry had taken over the principal functions of the Ministry of Agriculture.[84] However, under the Ministry of Finance land registration and assessment, and the actual collection of tax, remained as grossly inefficient as apparently it had been under the now defunct Ministry of Agriculture.[85] In March 1899 Rivett-Carnac proposed to Prince Mahit that responsibility for the administration of land registration, assessment and tax collection in the provinces be transferred to the Ministry of the Interior, for the latter's officials would have a far greater knowledge of conditions in the provinces than officials from a more exclusively Bangkok-based ministry.[86]

Prince Mahit supported the adviser's proposals.[87] But Prince Damrong was less enthusiastic. It was clear that if the Ministry of the Interior was to be responsible for both the administration of land in the provinces and the collection of the revenues upon it, and if, unlike the Ministry of Finance, it was to discharge those responsibilities effectively, then the provincial bureaucracy would face a considerable increase in work.[88] The matter was discussed between Prince Mahit, Prince Damrong and Rivett-Carnac in late July 1899,[89] and eventually a compromise emerged. The Ministry of Agriculture was re-established, responsible for land registration throughout the kingdom;[90] responsibility for the collection of land taxes in the provinces was given to the Ministry of the Interior, until such time as the Ministry of Agriculture could assume that task.[91] In late 1899 the *Krom Sanphākǫn Nǫk*, the Provincial Revenue Department, was established within the Ministry of the Interior. In 1900 the Bangkok and Provincial

Revenue Departments became responsible for the collection of the Chinese poll tax.[92] In the years which followed, an increasing number of taxes fell to those departments – including capitation taxes, gambling fees, pawnbroker licences, and fees to slaughter pigs.[93]

By the early years of the century, therefore, the Ministry of Finance had removed from itself responsibility for the actual collection of tax revenues within the kingdom. Indeed as early as 1897, its tax collection divisions, the *Krom Suai*, *Krom Sanphāsī*, *Krom Sanphākǭn*, were being broken up.[94] There were two basic factors behind this development. In the late 1890s the Ministry of Finance was struggling to control the expenditure ambitions of the administration. Prince Mahit did not want the effectiveness of the Ministry in that respect hampered by the burden of additional major responsibilities, responsibilities which, in any event, the Ministry would have found it extremely difficult to fulfil. Second, from its establishment in 1892, the Ministry of the Interior under Prince Damrong had been growing in effectiveness and influence, taking over some of the important provincial responsibilities – in the fields of justice, education, forestry and revenue – of the more Bangkok-focused ministries. It is possible to see this development as being in the tradition of the pre-reform administration – a powerful ministry attracting to itself an increasing range of functions, and in so doing blurring and confusing the functional differentiations within the administration structure.

A further influence may have encouraged the Ministry of Finance to divest itself of responsibility for the collection of these revenues. Briefly, the Ministry had to accept the tax structure as given, for the tax rates levied in Siam were, in effect, frozen by the treaties which had been signed with the western powers from the 1850s. Consequently it was possible to increase the amount of tax revenue raised in the kingdom only by working the existing structure more thoroughly and efficiently. Because it already had officials in the field, this was primarily a task for the Ministry of the Interior and, to a lesser extent, the Ministry of the Capital.

But whatever Prince Mahit's thinking in the late 1890s, to leave the Ministry of Finance with virtually no control over the collection of these major revenues could only weaken its control over the administration's expenditure, weaken its authority within the government. This is an important point which will be taken up in the concluding chapter.

Notes

1. Mahit to Chulalongkorn, 23 September 1896; 12 October 1896, NA r5 Kh 5.1/5.
2. Chulalongkorn to Mahit, 13 October 1896, NA r5 Kh 5.1/5.
3. Chulalongkorn to Čhao Phrayā Thēwētwongwiwat, 12 December 1896, NA r5 Kh 5.1/2.
4. Mahit to Sommot, 16 January 1897, NA r5 Kh 1/18. Similar letters were sent to all departments.
5. Mahit to Sommot, 18 March 1897, NA r5 Kh 1/18. Similar letters were sent to all departments.
6. Chulalongkorn to Mahit, 14 February 1897, NA r5 Kh 1/18.
7. Ibid.
8. Mahit to Chulalongkorn, 20 March 1897, NA r5 Kh 5.1/5.
9. Chulalongkorn to Sommot, 20 March 1897, NA r5 Kh 5.1/5.
10. Mahit to Chulalongkorn, 20 March 1897, NA r5 Kh 5.1/5. Unfortunately it is not until the year 1901/2 that there are detailed records of the budget discussions which took place in the Ministry of Finance and in the Council of Ministers. This means that for the earlier period there is no direct evidence as to the pace and extent to which the budget procedures introduced by the Ministry of Finance became effective. The fact that the Ministry felt it necessary to reissue its budget regulations virtually every year would suggest that any success it achieved in establishing effective procedures was relatively slow in coming.
11. Chulalongkorn to Mahit, 6 April 1897, NA r5 Kh 5.1/5.
12. Sī Sahathēp, *Raya thāng sadet phrarātchadamnōen praphāt prathēt yurōp r.s. 116* [The Royal Tour of Europe in 1897], Bangkok, n.d.
13. Ibid.
14. Mahit to Chulalongkorn, 1 February 1898, NA r5 Kh 5.1/5.
15. Mitchell-Innes to Chulalongkorn, 19 January 1898, NA r5 Kh 1/16.
16. Mahit to Chulalongkorn, 27 January 1898; Chulalongkorn to various ministers, 2 February 1898, NA r5 Kh 5.1/5.
17. Mahit to Chulalongkorn, 15 March 1898, NA r5 Kh 5.1/7.
18. Mahit to Chulalongkorn, 19 March 1898, NA r5 Kh 5.1/8.
19. Ibid.
20. Report on the meeting of the Council of Ministers, 26 March 1898, NA r5 Kh 5.1/8.

21. Ibid.
22. Ibid.
23. Mitchell-Innes to Sommot, 30 March 1898, NA r5 B 2Kh/424.
24. Mitchell-Innes to Chulalongkorn, 30 March 1898, NA r5 B 2Kh/424; Mitchell-Innes to Chulalongkorn, 3 April 1898, NA r5 Kh 5.1/10.
25. Mahit to Chulalongkorn, 20 April 1898, NA r5 Kh 5.1/8.
26. Chulalongkorn to Mahit, 23 April 1898, NA r5 Kh 5.1/8. It is again unfortunate that the National Archives contains no record of the budget discussions of the Council of Ministers, for that record would presumably illustrate the problems faced by the Ministry of Finance, as reported by Prince Mahit to the King. Yet the evidence which is available does support the Minister's argument. In 1898/9 the government had 29.13 million *baht* at its disposal: Mahit to Chulalongkorn, 20 April 1898, NA r5 Kh 5.1/8. This included the revenue returns for the year, plus unspent funds from 1897/8. As the ministries had originally requested 29.45 million *baht*, presumably few cuts in expenditure were necessary. In fact the total expenditure estimate for 1898/9 was 28.7 million *baht*. But actual expenditure in 1898/9 was only 23.78 million *baht*: *RFAB* 1903/4, p. 25. The ministries were asking for more funds than they were able to spend.
27. Mitchell-Innes to Chulalongkorn, 31 December 1898, NA r5 Kh 5.1/8.
28. Chulalongkorn to various ministers, 1 January 1899, NA r5 Kh 5.1/8.
29. Ibid.
30. Letters from various ministers to Chulalongkorn, early January 1899, NA r5 Kh 5.1/8.
31. *Bangkok Times*, 3 December 1898.
32. Rivett-Carnac memorandum, 28 December 1898, NA r5 Kh 5.1/8.
33. Chulalongkorn to Mahit, 3 January 1899, NA r5 Kh 5.1/8.
34. Mahit to Chulalongkorn, 13 February 1899, NA r5 B 2Kh.1/35.
35. Report of Committee, attached to Mahit to Chulalongkorn, 12 December 1899, NA r5 Kh 7/1.
36. Rivett-Carnac memorandum, 28 December 1898, NA r5 Kh 5.1/8.
37. Sommot to Rivett-Carnac, 1 July 1899, NA r5 Kh 7/1.
38. Rivett-Carnac to Sommot, 4 July 1899, NA r5 Kh 7/1.
39. Report of Committee, attached to Mahit to Chulalongkorn, 4 January 1900, NA r5 Kh 7/1.
40. Report of Committee, attached to Mahit to Chulalongkorn, 1 February 1900, NA r5 Kh 7/4.
41. Report of Committee, attached to Mahit to Chulalongkorn, 7 March 1900, NA r5 Kh 7/5.
42. Mahit to Chulalongkorn, undated, NA r5 Kh 5.1/11.
43. Mahit to Chulalongkorn, 11 April 1899, NA r5 Kh 5.1/11.
44. Memorandum upon the budget estimates for r.s. 118, Rivett-Carnac, 25 March 1899, NA r5 Kh 5.1/11.
45. Mahit to Chulalongkorn, 11 April 1899, NA r5 Kh 5.1/11.
46. Mahit to Chulalongkorn, 15 May 1899, NA r5 Kh 5.1/11.
47. Chulalongkorn to Mahit, 5 June 1899, NA r5 Kh 5.1/11.

48. Memorandum: financial position of the kingdom, Rivett-Carnac, 25 March 1899, NA r5 Kh 5.1/11.
49. Expenditure rose from 14.91 million *baht* in 1892/3 to 23.78 million *baht* in 1898/9: *RFAB* 1903/4, pp. 24–5.
50. *RFAB* 1903/4, p. 25.
51. A large number of these regulations are filed under NA r5 Kh 2 and NA K Kh 0301.1.29. Each set of regulations was produced in book-form and distributed to the appropriate divisions of the administration.
52. *RFAB* 1901/2, p. 18.
53. Mahit to Chulalongkorn, 21 March 1900, NA r5 Kh 5.1/11.
54. Chulalongkorn to Mahit, 1 April 1900, NA r5 Kh 5.1/11. It is important to note that actual government expenditure in 1900/1 was 31.84 million *baht* [*RFAB* 1903/4, p. 25] compared with the estimate of 32.66 million *baht* [Mahit to Chulalongkorn, 30 March 1900, NA r5 Kh 5.1/11], a shortfall of 820 000 *baht*. This compares with the figures for unspent funds of 5 million *baht* in 1898/9 and 3 million *baht* in 1899/1900. Once again this suggests that the administration was now producing more accurate and realistic expenditure estimates, and that the account and audit reforms being introduced by the Ministry of Finance were having some effect.
55. 1901/2 is also the first year for which the National Archives contains a record of the discussions between the Ministry of Finance and the other ministries over the preliminary expenditure estimates. Therefore some allowance must be made for the possibility that, to some extent, the apparent change in the nature of the Ministry's budget work simply reflects the arrival of this additional source material.
56. Report on discussion of budget estimates of Ministry of War, 26 March 1901, NA r5 Kh 5.1/14.
57. The following is taken from the reports of the budget discussions held in March–April 1901, NA r5 Kh 5.1/14.
58. Report of Committee, attached to Mahit to Chulalongkorn, 5 April 1901, NA r5 Kh 7/7.
59. Report of Committee, attached to Mahit to Chulalongkorn, 26 August 1901, NA r5 Kh 7/7.
60. Report of Committee, attached to Mahit to Chulalongkorn, 5 December 1901, NA r5 Kh 7/7.
61. Report of Committee, attached to Mahit to Chulalongkorn, 15 March 1902, NA r5 Kh 7/7.
62. Narit to Rivett-Carnac, 3 September 1902, NA r5 Kh 7/9.
63. Rivett-Carnac to Sommot, 9 December 1902, NA r5 Kh 7/9.
64. Chulalongkorn to Mahit, 17 December 1902, NA r5 Kh 7/9.
65. Report of Committee, attached to Mahit to Chulalongkorn, 16 March 1905, NA r5 Kh 7/9.
66. Mahit to Chulalongkorn, 19 April 1901, NA r5 Kh 5.1/14.
67. Chulalongkorn to Mahit, 27 April 1901, NA r5 Kh 5.1/14.
68. *RFAB* 1901/2, p. 2.
69. *RFAB* 1901/2, p. 1.

70. *RFAB* 1901/2, p. 18.
71. Memorandum: the publication of the budget, Rivett-Carnac, undated, NA r5 Kh 5.1/14.
72. Memorandum: communication of financial statement to Dr. Morrison, *The Times* correspondent, Rivett-Carnac, 18 April 1901, NA r5 Kh 5.1/16.
73. *The Times*, 7 September 1901.
74. Mahit to Chulalongkorn, 10 April 1902, NA r5 Kh 5.1/15.
75. *RFAB* 1902/3, p. 1.
76. Leaving out of account the year 1901/2, when the reserves were used to pay the unexpected compensation to Murray Campbell.
77. In 1900 the Bangkok spirit farmer ran into severe financial difficulties, and the Ministry of Finance was forced to re-auction the contract the following year: Mahit to Chulalongkorn, 13 July 1900, 24 February 1901, NA r5 Kh 14.1kh/20.
78. The first clause of the 1890 Act stated that the Ministry of Finance was to be responsible for, *inter alia*, 'collecting the taxes throughout the whole kingdom'.
79. Tej Bunnag, *The Provincial Administration of Siam 1892–1915. The Ministry of the Interior under Prince Damrong Rajanubhab*, Kuala Lumpur, 1977, p. 117.
80. Mahit to Chulalongkorn, 21 July 1898, NA r5 Kh 14.2/3. W. A. Graham, an Englishman, held a number of positions in the Siamese administration in this period, including in the 1900s the post of Siamese Adviser in Kelantan. He was the author of perhaps the best contemporary work of reference on the kingdom: *Siam: A Handbook of Practical, Commercial and Political Information*, which was first published in 1912.
81. Memorandum: remarks on the *khana*, W. A. Graham, July 1898, NA r5 Kh 14.2/3.
82. Mahit to Chulalongkorn, 21 July 1898; Chulalongkorn to Mahit, 29 July 1898, NA r5 Kh 14.2/3.
83. Memorandum, Rivett-Carnac, 18 March 1899, NA r5 Kh 14.1/2.
84. Mahit to Chulalongkorn, 30 March 1897, NA KS 1/3.
85. Memorandum, Rivett-Carnac, 18 March 1899, NA r5 Kh 14.1/2.
86. Ibid.
87. Mahit to Chulalongkorn, 29 June 1899, NA r5 Kh 14.1/2.
88. Damrong to Chulalongkorn, 18 July 1899, NA r5 Kh 14.1/2.
89. Mahit to Chulalongkorn, 28 July 1899, NA r5 Kh 14.1/2.
90. Chulalongkorn to Mahit, 2 September 1899, NA r5 Kh 14.1/2.
91. Damrong to Chulalongkorn, 9 September 1899, NA r5 Kh 14.1/4.
92. Damrong to Chulalongkorn, 4 May 1900, NA r5 Kh 13.1/6.
93. Statistics of the Provincial Revenue Department r.s. 121–133 (1902/3–1914/15), NA K Kh 0301.1.1/4; Report of the Bangkok Revenue Department r.s. 126 (1907/8), NA r5 Kh 14.1/7; Prince Damrong, *Ru'ang tamnān kānlōekbǫnbia lae lōek huai* [The Abolition of Gambling Dens and the Huai Lottery], Bangkok, 1960, p. 48. The total revenue collected by the Provincial Revenue Department rose from 8.113 million *baht* in 1902/3 to 18.559 million *baht* in 1910/11. In this

last year the Department was collecting some 30 per cent of the total revenue raised by government. The Bangkok Revenue Department collected less: 702 000 *baht* in 1899/1900 rising to 2.641 million *baht* in 1908/9 [that last figure is from Čhao Phrayā Yommarāt to Chulalongkorn, 1 December 1909, NA r5 Kh 14.1/7].

94. Mahit to Chulalongkorn, 30 March 1897, NA KS 1/3. After 1900 the only revenue collection division within the Ministry of Finance was the Customs Department.

4 The Effective Ministry in Operation: Financial Stringency, 1902–6

The last four years of Prince Mahit's term as Minister of Finance (from 1902 to 1906) saw the institution of a number of major reforms – notably the adoption of the gold-exchange standard and the beginning of the process which within a short period would see the abolition of the great revenue farms and the introduction of direct government administration of those revenues. I have considered these reforms elsewhere.[1] The present chapter, following the themes established earlier, will continue to focus on the development of the Ministry of Finance as an influential part of government, the relationships of the Ministry and its Minister with the rest of the administration. For the period 1902–1906, this primarily means an examination of the emergence of substantial budget deficits and the related issue of the raising of a loan in Europe.

4.1 BUDGET STRINGENCY AND THE FIRST EUROPEAN LOAN, 1902–6

Before considering in detail the debate which took place within the Siamese government from late 1902 to late 1904 over the raising of a loan in Europe, two preliminary points must be made. First, that loan was required to finance construction of the Siamese railway network, in particular the line from Bangkok to Chiangmai. Work on the first major line in the kingdom – from the capital north to Ayudhya and then north-east to Korat – had begun in the early 1890s. The Bangkok–Ayudhya section was opened in March 1897, the Ayudhya–Korat section in December 1900.[2] Continuation of the line north from Ayudhya towards Chiangmai was begun in mid-1898.[3] In this early period, construction was financed solely from current revenue. In the six years 1892/3–1898/9, 14.4 million *baht* was committed to railway construction, approximately ten per cent of total government expenditure in that period.[4] Second, the issue of the European loan could not be separated from that of Siam's political relations with the European powers. It need only be noted that this period saw the latter engaged in a scramble for concessions in China, a scramble that appeared as merely a prelude to the apparently inevitable disintegration of the Middle Kingdom. In this imperialist onslaught, the offering of loans to the Chinese government by the European powers and in return the granting of concessions to European interests to construct railways in China played a central part. The Siamese government was certainly aware of this. It could hardly be encouraged by it. In this respect it might be noted that the Hongkong and Shanghai Bank, a leading bank in the floating of Chinese loans, was also the principal western bank in Siam. Such considerations weighed heavily in Bangkok.

The first firm proposal that Siam raise a European loan appears to have been made by Mitchell-Innes in December 1897.[5] The following year the idea was discussed by the Council of Ministers, and as a result Prince Mahit was instructed to make enquiries in Europe as to the terms upon which a loan might be raised.[6] In February 1899 the British Minister in Bangkok reported to London that the Siamese government had decided to raise a loan of between £3 million and £5 million.[7] But on 28 August 1899 the *Bangkok Times* announced that the government had decided to postpone the raising of a loan in Europe, and that it would continue to finance railway construction from current revenue. The King apparently told Rivett-Carnac that although he had been in favour of the loan, his opinion had not prevailed.[8] It would seem that opposition came mainly from those ministers who feared the political complications of a foreign loan, but there were also practical problems. The government had yet to publish its annual budget and statement of accounts, a measure which Mitchell-Innes regarded as essential if European investors were to be made aware of Siam's recent financial, commercial and administrative progress – and therefore to be attracted to invest in a Siamese loan.[9] There was also the important point, made by Rivett-Carnac at about this time, that Siam should not raise a sterling loan while the *baht* remained on the silver standard, for with a depreciating currency against sterling, the burden of interest and capital repayments could increase enormously over the period of the loan.[10]

For two or three years after this decision to postpone the raising of a loan in Europe, the government was able, without serious difficulty, to continue to finance railway construction out of current revenue. In April 1900 a start was made on the Bangkok–Petchaburi line, and in May 1902 work was begun on the Lopburi–Paknampo section of the northern railway.[11] This was a substantial programme. By 1900/1 the government was investing 3.5 million *baht* each year in railway construction, which was more than double the figure for the early 1890s.[12] But in the budget for 1902/3 there were the first clear signs that this high level of expenditure from current revenue could not be maintained. In the estimates for that year, only 2 million *baht* of the 3.5 million *baht* allocated for railway construction was covered by current revenues: the balance was met from the treasury reserves.[13] Furthermore, in his report on the budget, produced in mid-1902, Rivett-Carnac announced that the allocation for railway construction would be cut to 3 million *baht* in 1903/4 and to 2 million *baht* in 1904/5.[14] It was clear that the policy of construction from current revenue was being surrendered. It was finally condemned by events in July 1902.

On 25 July 1902 a rebellion broke out in the northern town of Phrae.[15] It was led by some thirty to forty Shans who seized the town, occupied government offices and killed approximately twenty Siamese provincial officials. Immediately troops were despatched north from Phitsanulok and Nakon Sawan, but communications were extremely poor and it took several weeks for the government to muster sufficient strength in the area to put down the rising. Government troops re-occupied Phrae on 14 August. Although the Shan rising was a relatively limited affair, it greatly disturbed the government in Bangkok, for it exposed the weakness of its authority in that more distant part of the kingdom and therefore its vulnerability to the encroachments of the imperial powers. Perhaps the most disturbing feature of the rising, from the point of view of Bangkok, was the suspiciously close interest shown in it by the French and British consuls in nearby Nan. On 21 August 1902, one week after the collapse of the rebellion, King Chulalongkorn wrote to Prince Mahit to inform him that the government had decided to push ahead as quickly as possible with the construction of the northern railway as far as Uttaradit, the point at which it ran into the hills and only some 30 miles south of Phrae.[16] A programme of construction was agreed which called for a virtual doubling of the funds allocated to the Railway Department. It appeared to make a European loan unavoidable.

However, from December 1902 to March 1903 the government engaged in a detailed, often repetitious, debate over the probable balance of advantage and disadvantage in acquiring that loan. A considerable number of ministers and senior officials took part – Prince Mahit, Prince Devawongse, Prince Narit (the Minister of Public Works), Herr Gehrts (the German Director of the Railway Department) and Phrayā Suriyānuwat (the Siamese Minister in Paris). These participants divided into those who were at least sceptical with regard to the prospect of raising a foreign loan and those who clearly were in favour. The most dominant figure in the first group was Prince Devawongse, the Minister of Foreign Affairs. He pointed out that while the direct financial return on investment in railway construction in Siam had been around 3 per cent p.a., the government was almost certain to pay at least 5 per cent p.a. on a loan raised in Europe.[17] Behind this observation was Prince Devawongse's fear that the government might default on its loan, and thus provide an opportunity for the European powers to intervene. In short, he saw a European loan as a potential threat to Siamese independence. Prince Devawongse's misgivings were shared, and developed, by Prince

Narit and Herr Gehrts. They too were concerned that the direct return from railway construction was unlikely to reach 5 per cent p.a., under even the most favourable circumstances.[18] It was true, of course, that the railway would promote the commercial development of those parts of the kingdom through which it ran, and for this reason, argued the Director of the Railway Department, the direct financial return from railway construction could not be regarded as the sole, perhaps even the principal, return from that investment. But then it was important not to construct the railway too far ahead of the immediate commercial requirements of the kingdom.

> ... it is my opinion that the railways of this country ought not to be built too quickly. The spending of an average of 3.5 m. [*baht*] yearly as done in the years 117 [1898/9] to 120 [1901/2] is in general quite sufficient for the effective development of the country and will ensure a better financial result than the spending of larger sums.[19]

The point here was that if the government would accept a slower rate of construction and was prepared to terminate the line well south of Chiangmai, and assuming that the Railway Department was still allocated from the revenue 3.5 million *baht* each year for the coming six years, then it would be possible to continue the programme of railway construction without resorting to a European loan. Prince Narit supported this view, adding that even with a loan it would take five years to complete the northern railway. Which was better, he asked: to delay one year or to become indebted to European financiers?[20] Finally in this group was Phrayā Suriyā who, noting the poor direct return from the investment in railway construction, argued that the government would be better advised to use the proceeds of a European loan to establish a National Bank, specializing in agricultural loans.[21] The expansion of agricultural credit, he suggested, would act as a greater stimulus to cultivation – with all the benefits that that would bring to the government's revenues – than the construction of railways.

There was a major flaw in the arguments advanced by Prince Devawongse, Prince Narit, Herr Gehrts and Phrayā Suriyā. In late 1902 the government had decided for *political* reasons to push ahead with the construction of the northern railway: the arguments above had concentrated on the *commercial* considerations which would arise if that line were constructed by means of a European loan. In fairness, Phrayā Suriyā recognized this. In writing to Prince Devawongse in March 1903 he concluded: 'of course, if this railway policy is a political or strategical one then it must be carried out with all speed regardless of loss. And it does appear to be more of that than of a commercial nature'.[22]

The most forceful proponent of the European loan was Prince Mahit. However, in early 1903 his arguments were mainly defensive, countering those of the sceptics. He pointed out that the benefits to be derived from the construction of a railway network linking the capital with distant provinces were much broader than those suggested by narrow calculations of investment return. All the political and commercial advantages of improved communications – the encouragement of trade, the increase in revenues, the establishment of effective administration – had to be taken into account.[23] Prince Mahit also argued that it was no longer possible to finance railway construction from current revenue, even at the pre-1902 level of 3.5 million *baht* p.a., as the Ministry of Finance was now faced with rising demands for funds for other important projects – including the modernization of the army and the reconstruction of administration in the north in the wake of the Shan rebellion.[24] Indeed, as noted above, in the budget for 1902/3 the Ministry had been able to maintain the 3.5 million *baht* allocation for railway construction only by drawing 1.5 million *baht* from the reserves. That had been the position before the outbreak of the Shan rebellion, before the decision had been taken to increase expenditure on railway construction in order to push ahead rapidly with the laying down of the northern line as far as Uttaradit. In short, the choice was not between constructing the line quickly with a loan or slowly from current revenue, as

Prince Narit had argued. It was between constructing the line with a loan or abandoning the project entirely. Finally, the Minister of Finance considered the basic fear which troubled Prince Devawongse and possibly Prince Narit as well – the fear that a European loan would threaten Siamese sovereignty. It was true, he argued, that a foreign loan brought with it certain dangers. But there were also dangers in delaying a decision if the funds were urgently required.[25] That danger was the curtailment of the government's reform programme – which in itself would undermine the government's strategy to maintain independence.

At the same time as these opposing arguments were being advanced in Bangkok, initial enquiries were being made in Europe as to the terms upon which a loan might be raised. On 14 January 1903 Prince Mahit wrote to Phrayā Suriyā in Paris, outlining the conditions which the government would accept on a loan of £1 million, and suggesting that he find a reputable financier in Europe willing to assist in this matter.[26] Phrayā Suriyā was informed that he was also to be assisted by Rivett-Carnac, although the Minister was assured that he alone would conduct the main negotiations. In February 1903 the Financial Adviser left Bangkok for Europe, for the ill-health of Mrs. Rivett-Carnac required that she have a period away from the Siamese climate.[27] Before leaving Siam, Rivett-Carnac had strongly hinted to the British Minister that he, the adviser, would be negotiating the loan on behalf of Siam, and that he would like an interview with Lord Lansdowne, the Foreign Secretary, when he reached London.[28] At an interview at the Foreign Office in late March 1903 – although not with Lord Lansdowne – Rivett-Carnac suggested that when the time came for the Siamese government to raise its loan in Europe, although he had to 'make a show of inviting international competition...would do his utmost to secure that it should be actually placed in London'.[29] Prince Mahit was wise to entrust the loan negotiations to Phrayā Suriyā.

In April 1903 the government decided to postpone the decision on a European loan. The previous month the French Chamber of

Deputies had refused to ratify the Franco-Siamese treaty of 1902,[30] and with relations between the countries under strain it was felt by Phrayā Suriyā that a Siamese loan would receive little support in Paris.[31] And if the Siamese government turned to London for the whole of the loan, this would aggravate the discord between Bangkok and Paris. But for Prince Mahit, engaged in putting the final touches to the 1903/4 estimates, additional funds were desperately required.[32]

The Minister needed to finance three major projects – the modernization of the army (which involved an estimate of 3.74 million *baht* in 1903/4, some three and a half times the sum spent on the army in 1898/9);[33] the maintenance of forces in the north, which would include the costs of putting down the Shan rising; and the construction of the line to Uttaradit. The first two could be covered by the expansion in the revenue. The third – railway construction – could not. The Railway Department had requested 6 million *baht* in 1903/4 to continue the work on the northern railway. Prince Mahit could find only 1.5 million *baht* out of current revenue.[34] He telegraphed to Rivett-Carnac in Europe: how should the 4.5 million *baht* shortfall be covered?[35] Rivett-Carnac suggested that it be covered by the treasury reserves.[36] Prince Mahit was reluctant to draw further on the reserves.[37] The government could sell some of its European investments: again the Minister resisted. The only alternative was a European loan. In mid-June Rivett-Carnac telegraphed to Prince Mahit that the Hongkong and Shanghai Bank and the Chartered Bank were willing to underwrite a Siamese loan of £1 million at 5 per cent and 89 or 90 nett, once the market was favourable.[38]

On 7 July 1903 Prince Mahit wrote a long and very important letter to the King, reviewing the budget position facing the Ministry of Finance.[39] Most of the arguments advanced by the Minister were not new; the force with which they were expressed was. Prince Mahit began by emphasizing that the government was already committed to heavy investment in several public works projects. The sum of 19.6 million *baht* was required to construct the line to Uttaradit; to complete the line to Chiangmai would require a further 14.83 million *baht*. In addition, a Dutch irrigation expert, van der Heide, engaged in 1902, had just submitted his proposals for the construction of major irrigation facilities in the Chao Phraya plain.[40] There could be no question of the government finding from current revenue the funds to finance those two projects. It was Prince Mahit's fear that the Council of Ministers, instead of now proceeding with the European loan, would repeatedly postpone its decision, thus forcing the abandonment of those projects.

> If we wait [in proceeding with the public works projects] until we have the funds, then I must ask how many more eras will we wait: and then finally, where will the money come from?... I feel that in this matter, our mistake is that we hesitate. We do not make a quick, definite decision. In this situation...we will eventually collapse into confusion and disarray.[41]

Prince Mahit then outlined the terms offered by the London banks and reported by Rivett-Carnac. The effective rate of interest was just over 6 per cent p.a., which compared favourably with the terms recently obtained by China, Japan and Turkey. All the same, the Minister admitted, the government could expect, at best, a direct return of only 4 per cent p.a. from an investment in railway construction. However financial loss could be avoided. According to van der Heide, the irrigation schemes which he was proposing, by charging the farmer for irrigation water and by the sale of land newly opened up by irrigation works, would give a return on capital of 10 per cent p.a. Prince Mahit suggested that if a part of the European loan were to be invested in van der Heide's schemes, the high return there would compensate for the poor return on investment in the construction of the northern railway.

But the Minister of Finance always returned to his central theme. If there was further delay in raising a loan in Europe, the railway construction and irrigation projects would have to be abandoned – or at least severely curtailed. The Ministry of

Finance was already finding it necessary to draw on the reserves to keep the first of those projects in motion: if the current level of expenditure was continued without the support of a loan, the treasury would be bankrupt in 1904. Of that the Minister was certain.

It was an impassioned letter. Prince Mahit's annoyance, his frustration with the leisurely and frequently irrelevant debate being conducted by his colleagues, was overwhelmingly clear. The seriousness of the government's financial position was bluntly stated. Remarkably, the letter appears to have had little immediate effect.

The reply to Prince Mahit came from Prince Devawongse.[42] It was a disappointing letter, devoted largely to restatements of earlier points and to relatively trivial criticisms of Prince Mahit's numerical calculations. There were, however, one or two points of interest. First, with respect to van der Heide's irrigation proposals, Prince Devawongse suggested that the return on that investment, by way of the sale of irrigation water and of newly opened land, would not be as high as the Dutchman's report had stated and as Prince Mahit had accepted. In any event, the scale of the investment that was being proposed was far too ambitious.[43] The irrigation report should be abandoned and van der Heide replaced. There could be no question, therefore, of the return from investment in irrigation making good the poor return expected on the construction of the northern railway. Second, Prince Devawongse suggested that Prince Mahit had not seriously considered the alternative to raising a loan in Europe – a less ambitious programme of public works. He proposed that the government construct only those railway lines which would be directly profitable, with outlying areas being served by road and track. Prince Devawongse would still not acknowledge that the government was pushing ahead with the construction of the northern railway primarily for political and administrative reasons.

In his reply to Prince Devawongse, Prince Mahit could only restate that a European loan was urgently required if the government was to maintain its policy with respect to the construction of the northern railway.[44] It was evident that the Council of Ministers was seriously, almost irreconcilably, split. When the Council met on 13 August 1903, Prince Devawongse first attacked Prince Mahit, arguing that the Minister of Finance had published inadequate financial accounts, so that it was impossible to obtain reliable figures on the size of the reserves.[45] He then declared that 'while the revenues of the government are still sufficient to meet [the government's] needs, I do not think it would be appropriate...to rush out and borrow money from abroad as is being proposed here'.[46] That intervention was sufficient to prevent the government from reaching a decision. It appears that the King, in the absence of agreement, ordered the appointment of a committee of ministers to examine the government's various public works projects and consider how they were to be financed.[47] Decisions on the loan and on van der Heide's report were postponed. But it was decided to continue with the rapid construction of the line to Uttaradit. The allocation of 6 million *baht* to the Railway Department was confirmed, with 4.5 million *baht* to come from the treasury reserves.[48] A further 3 million *baht* was to be drawn from the reserves to cover part of the army's expenditure allocation.[49]

To appreciate the full consequences of those decisions it is necessary to refer briefly to another issue – the management of the kingdom's exchange mechanism. In November 1902 Siam had abandoned the silver standard and adopted a gold-exchange standard.[50] Under the new exchange mechanism, the Ministry of Finance had to ensure that the treasury held sufficient reserves of *baht* coin to meet all the demands of the Bangkok banks that would arise in the financing of external trade. Were the Ministry to fail in that obligation, the kingdom's trade could be brought to a halt. In November 1903 Rivett-Carnac, now returned from leave in Europe, submitted a memorandum to Prince Mahit on the government's cash reserves.[51] He argued that the administration could not allow the reserves to fall below 22 million *baht* without endangering trade. In November 1903 they were down to 18 million *baht*, and the 4.5 million *baht* now set aside for railway construction in 1903/4 had still to be withdrawn. It was possible that by March 1904 the cash balances could be as low as 12 million *baht*. In order to prevent further falls in the level of cash reserves, Rivett-Carnac recommended a series of quite drastic measures. He proposed that there be no increase in allocations above the funds already sanctioned in the budget – in particular, that there be no additional expenditure on irrigation:

> Before we can think of a great Irrigation Scheme, we must provide funds for the strategic Railways which are essential if the outlying Provinces are to be properly governed. Those railways must be constructed out of borrowed capital and I am altogether averse to borrowing money for Irrigation at present, in addition to money for Railway Construction. Such a course would be rash in the extreme.[52]

The Financial Adviser proposed that in future all expenditure on the armed forces be met entirely from current revenue; and that all ministers be forcefully reminded, again, to maintain the most strict control over their expenditures.

Prince Mahit wrote again to the King in December 1903.[53] The Minister's immediate objective was to obtain approval for the withdrawal of a further 3.4 million *baht* from the reserves to cover the projected budget deficit for 1903/4. But his principal aim was once again to draw the King's attention to the government's increasingly dangerous financial position, particularly to the alarming rate at which the reserves were disappearing. The King called a meeting of senior ministers – Prince Damrong, Prince Devawongse and Prince Mahit – although for reasons which are not clear the last was unable to attend.[54] The further withdrawal from the treasury was approved.[55] But there was no acknowledgment of the wider issue.

However the matter was now moving towards a climax. In May 1904 Prince Mahit was working on the budget estimates for 1904/5. Because of heavy expenditure demands from, in particular, the Ministry of the Interior,[56] and from the army and the navy, there was a projected deficit of 9.889 million *baht*.[57]

Consequently the full expenditure allocation of the Railway Department (6 million *baht*) and the full cost of constructing a new arsenal for the army (3.9 million *baht*) were to be met from the reserves. This implied a drop in the reserves of almost one half over the year. If during that year, Prince Mahit warned, the government was faced with a sudden crisis – the collapse of a major revenue farm, an unexpected call for further expenditure – it would be in very serious trouble. Certainly the government would not be able to satisfy the demands of the banks for *baht*. The estimates and the treasury withdrawals were sanctioned by the King – apparently without comment.[58]

In a further letter to the King on 8 June 1904, Prince Mahit argued that by the end of the financial year (31 March 1905) the reserves would be down to 10 million *baht* and, if the current level of expenditure was then maintained, would disappear altogether in 1906 or 1907.[59] There was absolutely no alternative, he urged, but to raise a loan in Europe. The King then wrote to Prince Damrong to ask whether the committee established in August 1903 to examine the financing of the government's public works projects had completed its discussions.[60] Prince Damrong replied that it had not: and he then argued that this issue, in effect whether or not Siam should raise a loan in Europe, could not be separated from the matter of Siam's political relations with the European powers, and therefore that the opinion of the General Adviser, Edward Strobel, should be sought.[61] The King agreed, and the relevant documents were sent to Strobel.[62]

Clearly the decision to refer the matter to the General Adviser was taken not because the European loan was a political issue, although of course it was, but rather in order to attempt to break the deadlock in the Council of Ministers. That deadlock must, by this time, have driven Prince Mahit close to despair. Given the reform programme that the government had set itself (in particular the rapid construction of the northern railway and the modernization of the army) and the financial constraints that it had accepted (the required level of cash balances), the Minister's case was simply unanswerable. Yet after almost two years the

Council of Ministers remained divided and thus paralysed. Prince Mahit lacked the political weight to overcome the opposition of his cautious colleagues, despite the fact that the King himself appears to have been in favour of the loan. At the suggestion of Prince Damrong, therefore, the government appealed outside its own inner ranks, to a foreign adviser. Strobel's major qualification in these circumstances was that he was impartial; he was an American (no American bank was likely to take an interest in a Siamese loan) and he was not attached to the Ministry of Finance. In contrast, the only other outsiders to whom the Council might have turned, Rivett-Carnac and his successor, Williamson, were both British (the Hongkong and Shanghai Bank was certain to be involved in the loan) and were both employed in the Ministry of Finance.

Strobel submitted his report on 25 October 1904.[63] He pointed out that when the prospect of a loan had first been raised, that is in late 1902, it had been possible to argue that the northern railway could be constructed from current revenue, although with a European loan construction would, of course, be far quicker. By 1904 the financial situation had radically altered. The government had run into a series of severe budget deficits, and was finding it impossible to finance its public works projects from current revenue – witness the fact that in 1904/5 the entire allocation for railway construction had had to come from the reserves. Therefore a loan was now essential if construction of the northern railway, to name the most prominent project, was to continue. Strobel then referred to Rivett-Carnac's November 1903 memorandum which had advocated a minimum cash reserve of 22 million *baht*; in October 1904 the reserves stood at 16.2 million *baht*. But the General Adviser also had a word of encouragement for those ministers who feared the political dangers of raising a loan in Europe:

> The states which become involved in serious difficulties are those... which borrow money with great recklessness, spend it with great recklessness and thereby become exposed to the intervention of foreign powers on behalf of their subjects who

> have loaned money and are unable to obtain any settlement. If, however, loans are made only because absolutely necessary and well within the capacity of the country to meet its obligations and with a proper financial administration, there is no danger resulting from a foreign loan; and it is only on the assumption that these conditions exist (as I believe they do) in Siam that I proceed to discuss the question.[64]

Within a few days, Strobel's memorandum was supported by one from Williamson, now Financial Adviser:

> ...the loan has now become an absolute necessity, as the drain from the reserves which has been taking place for the last seven months has already weakened it very considerably, and if this is allowed to continue much longer, the financial administration of the Government will be in serious danger.[65]

This was plain speaking from both Strobel and Williamson, made more effective by the fact that neither was prone to exaggeration. But their arguments were not new. Prince Mahit had been making exactly the same points, with equal emphasis, for over a year.

The Council of Ministers met on 18 November 1904.[66] The meeting was dominated by the King who argued that the case for the loan had been established beyond doubt. Prince Devawongse merely sought an assurance from the Minister of Finance that Siam would be able to meet all the charges on the loan. In short the King, armed with Strobel's memorandum, broke the deadlock. Prince Mahit and Prince Devawongse were now charged with raising the loan, with the actual negotiations being entrusted to Phrayā Suriyā in Paris.

In early 1905, when negotiations could begin in earnest, the principal competitor for the loan was a partnership of the Hongkong and Shanghai Bank and the Banque de l'Indochine.[67] However Phrayā Suriyā began by inviting offers from banks in Belgium, Switzerland, Holland, Denmark and Germany. The response was discouraging. Each bank required either the customs revenue or the completed section of the railway as security.[68] Rivett-Carnac then approached the Hongkong and Shanghai Bank, but it offered only 92 nett at 5 per cent, although with no security.[69]

On 30 January 1905 Phrayā Suriyā wrote to Axel Johnson, the Siamese consul in Stockholm, to ask for assistance.[70] Johnson had been involved in earlier enquiries. The consul immediately contacted a business associate, K.A. Wallenberg, a prominent Stockholm banker who had been involved in floating a large number of public loans in Scandinavia. The three men – Phrayā Suriyā, Johnson and Wallenberg – met in Paris on 13 February and began negotiations with the Hongkong and Shanghai Bank and the Banque de l'Indochine, now in partnership. Within three days agreement had been reached. The banks offered 90½ nett at 4½ per cent. It was understood that the Danske Landmannsbank, of which Wallenberg was a director, would underwrite a small part of the loan. Phrayā Suriyā immediately telegraphed to Bangkok, asking for permission to close the negotiations with those terms.[71] Prince Mahit favoured acceptance.[72] Phrayā Suriyā was on the spot, and if he felt that the best possible terms had been secured then his judgement had to be accepted. The King and then the Council of Ministers agreed.[73]

The final details of the loan contract were negotiated in London by Phrayā Suriyā and Rivett-Carnac, now the Financial Agent in Europe, and the contract was signed on 19 March.[74] The loan was for £1 million, bearing interest at 4½ per cent and issued at 95½. It could be redeemed by the Siamese government after 10 years but had to be repaid after no more than 40 years. It was secured on the general credit of the kingdom. The loan was issued on 24 March 1905, and within one hour the lists were closed,[75] the issue being over-subscribed eight times.[76] 'The credit of Siam has been instantaneously and firmly established and has proved to be much better than that of any other Asian Power', boasted Rivett-Carnac.[77]

Several minor factors contributed to this success. A relatively small sum had been borrowed, and therefore the possibility that Siam might be unable to service the loan on schedule was slight. Second, the London and Paris banks had agreed to reduce the rate of interest from 5 per cent to 4½ per cent through fear, unwarranted as it turned out, of German competition for the loan.[78] Third, in early March 1905 the British authorities had reduced Bank Rate from 3 per cent to 2½ per cent, and this had made Siamese stock that much more attractive to London investors.[79] But there can be little doubt that the principal factor to account for the success of Siam's first loan was, as Prince Mahit put it, that 'the careful financial administration of the past few years and the policy of publishing an annual statement of the budget figures, have not been without their effect on financial circles in Europe'.[80] The awareness on the part of European investors of the recent progress in Siam's financial administration might also explain why the loan carried no specific security. The banks and investors were confident that Siam would meet all its loan charges and would use the proceeds of the loan prudently. Here it is important to note that the employment by the Siamese government of a British financial adviser, a man who, if one judged from his published reports on the budget, held considerable influence in Siam, probably did much to reassure British investors. Nor should the influence of the frequent reports in *The Times* by the paper's Peking correspondent on the current progress of the kingdom, or the influence of such favourable contemporary books on Siam as that by Cecil Carter,[81] be underestimated.

The success of the loan was regarded as a personal triumph for Phrayā Suriyā. In April 1905 he returned to Bangkok at the end of his term as Siamese Minister in Paris, and was presented with the First Class Order of Merit and a 'magnificent' residence by the King.[82] The Council of Ministers voted him 40,000 *baht* in recognition of his services in Paris. In June 1905 he replaced Prince Narit as Minister of Public Works.[83] Within a year he was Minister of Finance.

The full proceeds of the 1905 loan came to £905 000, equivalent to 14.5 million *baht*.[84] Immediately the 6 million *baht* drawn from the reserves to meet the expenditure allocation of the Railway Department in 1904/5 was repaid to the treasury.[85] A further 5.8 million *baht* was set aside for railway construction in 1905/6, so that in that year no part of the expenditure of the

Railway Department would be covered by current revenue. The remaining proceeds were invested in German and Egyptian stock until they were required.[86]

There was little of note in the budget estimates for 1905/6. The estimates, showing a small revenue surplus, were approved by the Council on 20 May 1905 without discussion or comment.[87] However, the compilation of the budget for 1906/7 brought familiar problems. The Railway Department was allocated 7.25 million *baht*, but no part of this sum could be met from current revenue. At the same time, after the large allocations to the Department in the preceding two years, only 5.8 million *baht* was left from the proceeds of the 1905 loan. Once again the Minister of Finance was forced to draw on the reserves to cover the expenditure on the government's major public works project.[88] In April 1906 Prince Mahit wrote to the King to argue that within a year the government would have to raise a further loan.[89] But this was to be a problem for Prince Mahit's successor.

4.2 REVENUE AND THE CLOSING OF THE GAMBLING DENS

From the mid-1890s the government had enjoyed a rapid growth in its revenue, achieved partly as a result of improved administration and improved methods of tax collection, partly as a result of a sustained increase in the level of economic activity in the kingdom. This rapid growth continued into the following decade. Between 1902/3 and 1906/7, government revenue rose from 39.15 million *baht* to 57.01 million *baht*.[90] It was against that background that the Ministry of Finance took steps to abolish one of the principal sources of revenue – the gambling farms.

The policy of closing down the gambling dens had been initiated by Prince Narāthip in the late 1880s. However his closures had been limited to the Bangkok area. It was not until 1898 that attention was focused on the dens outside the capital. In May of that year, Prince Damrong and Prince Mahit decided to abolish all the provincial gambling farms where the revenue was small or where the existence of the dens was found to be encouraging crime.[91] At the annual meetings of the provincial governors in Bangkok in 1899 and 1900, the closure of additional dens was agreed.[92] But the effect of these closures was simply to bring gambling under greater control – to restrict it to a relatively few, tightly regulated establishments. There is little evidence that the restrictionist policy pursued in this period reduced the amount of legal gambling carried on in the kingdom. The high level of Chinese immigration during these years – that alone – would have implied an increase. And indeed, the government's revenue from gambling rose from 1.832 million *baht* in 1892/3 to 5.244 million *baht* in 1900/1.[93] But it was also clear that at some point the restrictionist policy would begin to bite – that the continued closing of gambling dens would lead to a reduction in the level of legal gambling and in the revenue. In the early 1900s Prince Mahit felt that that point had been reached.

In August 1903 Prince Damrong proposed that the government consider reducing the number of provincial gambling farms, if not abolishing them entirely.[94] This proposal was discussed by the Minister of the Interior with Prince Mahit over a period of some fifteen months,[95] until finally, on 15 December 1904, they presented their views to the Council of Ministers.[96] As was to be expected, Prince Mahit was concerned that it would be difficult to find alternative sources of revenue to compensate for the loss of this income – approximately 4 million *baht* each year. Prince Damrong suggested that additional revenue could be raised through an increase in the rates of land tax. In fact the Minister of the Interior wished to see the Bangkok gambling dens closed at the same time as those in the provinces, otherwise, he argued, every gambler and criminal in the kingdom would move into the capital once the provincial dens disappeared. The loss of revenue in closing the Bangkok dens – approximately 3 million *baht* each year – would be made good, Prince Damrong suggested, through an increase in import duties. This would require the agreement of the treaty powers. Prince Mahit was very reluctant to agree to the closing of the Bangkok dens. The sudden removal of all opportunities for legal gambling throughout the kingdom would be certain to disturb the Chinese population and could lead to riots. The Council of Ministers decided to defer the decision on the Bangkok dens but to proceed with the abolition of those in the provinces.[97]

Immediately Prince Damrong instructed F.C. Giles, the head of the Provincial Revenue Department, to prepare proposals for raising additional revenue from the land tax, to replace that to be lost by the abolition of the provincial dens.[98] In this, the Siamese government was to take advantage of the provisions of the Land Tax Agreement signed with Britain in September 1900, under which Britain had agreed to the abolition of the 'Schedule of Taxes on Garden-Ground, Plantations, or Other Lands' attached to the Supplementary Agreement drawn up with Sir Harry Parkes in May 1856 (the effect of the Schedule had been to freeze the level and structure of land taxation in Siam, preventing the government from securing more than a small, and indeed diminishing, proportion of the value of agricultural output), in return for an undertaking from the Siamese government that its rates of land tax would not exceed the rates in force in Lower Burma. In 1905 Giles proposed that agricultural land be divided into six classes according to its fertility, the price of rice in local markets, the ease of transport to the market, and the distance from rice mills. The rates of tax would rise from a minimum of 24 *atts* per *rai* (the maximum rate under the old system) to 1 *baht* per *rai,* with approximately half the agricultural land in the kingdom being taxed at the top rate.[99] Giles estimated that under the new structure, the land tax would secure 6.2 million *baht* each year, an increase of 3.7 million *baht* on the existing annual yield.

Giles' proposals for the land tax and the proposed abolition of the gambling dens were discussed within the administration in late 1904 and early 1905.[100] It was decided that in 1905/6 all provincial dens which yielded less than 50 000 *baht* would be closed; the remaining provincial dens would be closed in 1906/7. The Bangkok dens would be abolished in 1907/8. At the suggestion of Prince Damrong, the closing of the Bangkok dens would be linked to an application to the treaty powers for a relaxation of the restrictions imposed on the kingdom's foreign trade duties. In that way, if the western powers refused to allow an increase in the trade duties they, and not the Siamese government, would be responsible for the continued existence of gambling dens in Bangkok. On 18 January 1905 Strobel was instructed to prepare for an approach to the treaty powers.[101]

In 1905/6 all save 22 provincial dens were closed, and the number of Bangkok dens was reduced to 13.[102] In many provinces the closing of the gambling dens was cause for several days of public celebration, often led by the provincial governor.[103] Messages were received from anti-gambling leagues and from missionary societies throughout the world.[104] The last of the provincial dens was closed, as planned, during the year 1906/7. Inevitably the government's revenue from gambling dropped dramatically, from 6.87 million *baht* in 1904/5 to 3.6 million *baht* in 1906/7. But, as was intended, that reduction was easily covered by the increase in the revenue from the land tax, which rose from 4.72 million *baht* in 1905/6 to 8.37 million *baht* in 1906/7, and to 8.56 million *baht* in 1907/8.[105] There remained the 13 dens in the capital.

In January 1906 the western powers were given notice of the Siamese government's intention to renegotiate the commercial treaties.[106] In reply to the Siamese note, the French administration made it clear that it would require a substantial *quid pro quo*: for example Siam might consider some concession over Battambang.[107] When the Siamese note was received in London in February 1906, the British administration too prepared a list of possible *quid pro quo*: the granting to British subjects of the right to hold land in the Chiangmai area, the dredging of the bar at the mouth of the Chao Phraya river, an undertaking not to increase export duties.[108]

But Siam did not put formal proposals to the powers. When Strobel visited London in January 1907, there is no record that the matter was discussed.[109] However when the adviser returned to Bangkok he suggested to the British Minister that an undertaking to allow for an increase in import duties might be worked into a larger agreement by which the Siamese Malay States would be transferred to Britain.[110] It would appear that when the Siamese authorities realized that each of the western powers would demand substantial concessions from Siam in return for a renegotiation of the commercial treaties, it was decided to abandon the strategy arrived at in early 1905.[111] Taken together, those concessions would have constituted too great a sacrifice on the part of Siam. And the negotiations themselves, involving different concessions to different powers, would have been impossibly complex.

This meant, of course, that the gambling dens in Bangkok remained open beyond 1907/8. The point had been put firmly by Williamson a few years earlier:

> State regulated gambling is, doubtless, indefensible on moral and other grounds, but the practical administrator has to take facts as he finds them...The question in Siam is entirely one of ways and means, and the Government, having once put its hand to the plough in the matter of progress on modern lines, cannot afford for merely sentimental considerations, to cripple the administration by voluntarily surrendering so large a portion of its annual income as the abolition of the Gambling Farms would entail.[112]

However it was only a matter of a few years before the Siamese government found the 'ways and means' to complete the reform initiated by Prince Narāthip in the late 1880s. The number of Bangkok gambling dens was reduced from 13 to 11 in 1909/10, and then to 9 in 1910/11.[113] In 1911/12 the number of dens was cut to 5.[114] According to W.A. Graham, at about this time an anti-gambling league was formed in Siam to press for the abolition of the few remaining gambling dens, and for the abolition of the important farmed lottery, the *Huai*.[115] In 1913/14 and 1914/15 there were large budget surpluses, amounting to almost 20 million *baht*, and the government took the opportunity to abolish the lottery in April 1916.[116] The remaining Bangkok gambling dens were closed in April 1917.[117]

4.3 THE RESIGNATION OF PRINCE MAHIT, MAY 1906

Prince Mahit resigned as Minister of Finance at the end of May 1906.[118] In the preceding two weeks he had been the focus of a diplomatic inquiry that arose from his close involvement in the establishment and initial operation of a banking institution, the 'Book Club', later to become the Siam Commercial Bank.[119] In mid-May 1906 the British Minister in Bangkok informally alleged that Prince Mahit had used his official position to transfer government balances held at the British banks to the new institution, and, furthermore, had used his influence to induce customers of the British banks to move their business to the new bank. These allegations severely disturbed Prince Mahit, for at one point they threatened to provoke a more serious diplomatic crisis. Perhaps more importantly, they brought further strain to a man whose health had long been poor (he had been forced to seek leave of absence earlier in 1906)[120] and who had already carried the crushing burden of his position for almost a decade. The official announcement of his resignation gave as the reason the Minister's ill-health.[121] In a little under a year Prince Mahit was dead. He died, of consumption, on 15 April 1907, at the age of 44.[122]

Notes

1. Ian Brown, 'Siam and the Gold Standard, 1902–1908', *Journal of Southeast Asian Studies*, 10, 2 (September 1979), pp. 381–99; Ian Brown, 'The End of the Opium Farm in Siam, 1905–07', in John Butcher, Jennifer Cushman and Howard Dick (eds.), *The Rise and Fall of Revenue Farming in South-East Asia*, London [forthcoming].
2. Thailand, Royal State Railways, *Report on the Traffic of the Nagara Rajasima Railway r.s. 116 (1897/98); Report on the Traffic of the Royal Siamese State Railways r.s. 119 (1900/01).*
3. Moss Blundell to Bertie, 15 July 1898, PRO FO 69/185.
4. *RFAB* 1903/4, pp. 24–5.
5. Memorandum on the negotiation of a loan, Mitchell-Innes, 28 December 1897, NA K Kh 0301.1.25/22.
6. Chalōem Yongbunkōet, 'Ngoenkū khrangrāek khǭng prathētthai'

[Thailand's First Loan], *Wārasān krombanchīklāng*, May 1961, pp. 43–51.
7. Greville to Salisbury, 27 February 1899, PRO FO 69/195.
8. Greville to Salisbury, 30 August 1899, PRO FO 69/196.
9. Memorandum on the negotiation of a loan, Mitchell-Innes, 28 December 1897, NA K Kh 0301.1.25/22.
10. Note: object of and reasons for establishing a gold standard for Siam, Rivett-Carnac, 9 September 1899, NA K Kh 0301.1.23/1.
11. Thailand, Royal State Railways, *Report on the Traffic of the Royal Siamese State Railways r.s. 122 (1903/04); Report on the Traffic of the Royal Siamese State Railways r.s. 124 (1905/06).*
12. *RFAB* 1903/4, pp. 24–5.
13. *RFAB* 1902/3, p. 14.
14. Ibid.
15. Tej Bunnag, 'Khabotngiao mu'angphrāe r.s. 121' ['The 1902 Shan Rebellion at Phrae'], *Sangkhomsāt parithat*, 6, 2 (September–November 1968), pp. 67–80; David F. Holm, 'The Role of the State Railways in Thai History, 1892–1932'. PhD diss., Yale University, 1977, pp. 113–15.
16. Mahit to Chulalongkorn, 18 December 1902, NA r5 Kh 25/1.
17. Devawongse to Chulalongkorn, 24 December 1902, NA r5 Kh 25/3.
18. Gehrts to Narit, 20 January 1903, NA r5 Kh 25/3.
19. Ibid.
20. Narit to Chulalongkorn, 2 February 1903, NA r5 Kh 25/3.
21. Phrayā Suriyā to Devawongse, 13 March 1903, NA K Kh 0301.1.25/1.
22. Ibid.
23. Mahit to Chulalongkorn, 25 December 1902, NA r5 Kh 25/1.
24. Mahit to Chulalongkorn, 5 February 1903, NA r5 Kh 25/3.
25. Ibid.
26. Mahit to Phrayā Suriyā, 14 January 1903, NA r5 Kh 25/3.
27. Mahit to Chulalongkorn, 25 December 1902, NA r5 Kh 25/1.
28. Paget to Lansdowne, 2 February 1903; Paget to Langley, 11 February 1903, PRO FO 69/245.
29. Memorandum: interview with Mr. Rivett-Carnac, Campbell, 23 March 1903, PRO FO 69/250.
30. Phrayā Suriyā to Devawongse, 16 March 1903, NA r5 Kh 25/3.
31. Phrayā Suriyā to Devawongse, 21 March 1903, NA K Kh 0301.1.25/1.
32. Mahit to Rivett-Carnac, 28 April 1903, NA r5 Kh 25/3.
33. *RFAB* 1901/2 p. 22; *RFAB* 1903/4, p. 21.
34. Mahit to Chulalongkorn, 4 May 1903, NA r5 Kh 5.1/18.
35. Mahit to Rivett-Carnac, 28 April 1903, NA r5 Kh 25/3.
36. Rivett-Carnac to Mahit, 1 May 1903, NA r5 Kh 25/3.
37. Mahit to Rivett-Carnac, 30 May 1903, NA r5 Kh 25/3. Between June 1902 and June 1903 the *baht* reserves of the Ministry of Finance fell from 9.3 million to 3.7 million: biannual reports from Mahit to Chulalongkorn regarding the size of the treasury reserves, NA r5 Kh 7/8.
38. Rivett-Carnac to Mahit, 17 June 1903, 24 June 1903, NA r5 Kh 25/3.
39. Mahit to Chulalongkorn, 7 July 1903, NA r5 Kh 25/3.

40. J. Homan van der Heide, *General Report on Irrigation and Drainage in the Lower Menam Valley*, Bangkok, 1903.
41. Mahit to Chulalongkorn, 7 July 1903, NA r5 Kh 25/3.
42. Devawongse to Chulalongkorn, 18 July 1903, NA r5 Kh 25/3.
43. For a detailed examination of van der Heide's proposals and of the government's response to them, see Ian Brown, *The Élite and the Economy in Siam c. 1890–1920*, Singapore, 1988, chapter 1.
44. Mahit to Chulalongkorn, 28 July 1903, NA r5 Kh 25/3.
45. Mahit to Chulalongkorn, 14 August 1903; Devawongse to Chulalongkorn, 24 August 1903, NA r5 Kh 5.1/19.
46. Devawongse to Chulalongkorn, 24 August 1903, NA r5 Kh 5.1/19.
47. Unfortunately the only source for this meeting of the Council is Prince Devawongse's letter to the King (24 August 1903, NA r5 Kh 5.1/19). Nor is there further information on the committee, apart from a reference in June 1904 (Note by Chulalongkorn, 10 June 1904, NA r5 Kh 25/7) which stated that it comprised Prince Mahit, Prince Devawongse, Prince Damrong, Prince Narit and Čhao Phrayā Thēwēt, and that at that point – June 1904 – it had yet to complete its work.
48. *RFAB* 1903/4, p. 12.
49. Williamson to Rivett-Carnac, 29 August 1903, NA K Kh 0301.1.25/1.
50. See Ian Brown, 'Siam and the Gold Standard, 1902–1908', *Journal of Southeast Asian Studies*, 10, 2 (September 1979), pp. 381–99.
51. Memorandum by the Financial Adviser upon the cash balances of the government, Rivett-Carnac, 25 November 1903, NA K Kh 0301.1.30/6.
52. Ibid.
53. Mahit to Chulalongkorn, 19 December 1903, NA r5 Kh 5.1/21.
54. Sommot to Mahit, 16 January 1904, NA r5 Kh 5.1/21.
55. Chulalongkorn to Mahit, 26 January 1904, NA r5 Kh 5.1/21.
56. The allocation for the Ministry of the Interior in 1904/5 was 10.988 million *baht*, compared with an actual expenditure in 1903/4 of 6.588 million *baht*: *RFAB* 1905/6, p. 18.
57. Mahit to Chulalongkorn, 9 May 1904, NA r5 Kh 5.1/22.
58. Chulalongkorn to Mahit, 17 May 1904, NA r5 Kh 5.1/22.
59. Mahit to Chulalongkorn, 8 June 1904, NA r5 Kh 25/7.
60. Note by Chulalongkorn, 10 June 1904, NA r5 Kh 25/7.
61. Damrong to Chulalongkorn, 17 June 1904, NA r5 Kh 25/7.
62. Chulalongkorn to Damrong, 22 June 1904, NA r5 Kh 25/7.
63. Memorandum by the General Adviser on the question of the loan, Strobel, 25 October 1904, NA r5 Kh 25/5.
64. Ibid.
65. Memorandum: proposed loan for railway construction, Williamson, 1 November 1904, NA K Kh 0301.1.25/1.
66. Report on the meeting of the Council of Ministers, 18 November 1904, NA r5 Kh 25/8.
67. In June 1904 Phrayā Suriyā had asked the French bank whether it would consider underwriting a Siamese loan. The bank consulted its government and then decided to share the loan with the Hongkong and

Shanghai Bank (Beckett to Lansdowne, 4 October 1904, PRO FO 69/255). The London bank, after consulting the Foreign Office (Cameron to Campbell, 10 June 1904, PRO FO 69/260), accepted the arrangement.

68. Phrayā Suriyā to Devawongse, 23 March 1905, NA r5 Kh 25/5.
69. Rivett-Carnac to Mahit, 10 March 1905; Phrayā Suriyā to Devawongse, 28 February 1905, NA r5 Kh 25/5.
70. Johnson to Devawongse, 18 April 1905, NA r5 Kh 25/5.
71. Phrayā Suriyā to Devawongse, 16 February 1905, NA r5 Kh 25/5.
72. Mahit to Chulalongkorn, 25 February 1905, NA r5 Kh 25/5.
73. Chulalongkorn to Mahit, 26 February 1905, NA r5 Kh 25/5; Report on the meeting of the Council of Ministers, 27 February 1905, NA r5 Kh 25/8.
74. Phrayā Suriyā to Devawongse, 9 March 1905; Johnson to Devawongse, 18 April 1905, NA r5 Kh 25/5.
75. Rivett-Carnac to Mahit, 24 March 1905, NA r5 Kh 25/5.
76. *RFAB* 1905/6, p. 7.
77. Rivett-Carnac to Mahit, 24 March 1905, NA r5 Kh 25/5.
78. Memorandum: Siamese loan of £1.0 million, Campbell, 9 March 1905, PRO FO 69/269. The banks had originally intended to offer Siam 87 or 88 nett at 5 per cent (Beckett to Lansdowne, 4 October 1904, PRO FO 69/255).
79. Rivett-Carnac to Mahit, 10 March 1905, NA r5 Kh 25/5.
80. Mahit to Rivett-Carnac, 4 May 1905, NA K Kh 0301.1.25/1.
81. A. Cecil Carter, *The Kingdom of Siam*, New York, 1904.
82. *Bangkok Times*, 1 June 1906.
83. *Bangkok Times*, 15 June 1905.
84. *RFAB* 1905/6, p. 7.
85. Mahit to Chulalongkorn, 17 May 1905, NA r5 Kh 5.1/24.
86. Mahit to Rivett-Carnac, 11 May 1905, NA K Kh 0301.1.25/1.
87. Report on the meeting of the Council of Ministers, 20 May 1905, NA r5 Kh 5.1/24.
88. Mahit to Chulalongkorn, 18 April 1906, NA r5 Kh 5.1/25.
89. Ibid.
90. Over the period 1892/3 to 1911/12, the government's revenue (in *baht* millions) increased as follows: 1892/3, 15.37; 1896/7, 20.64; 1901/2, 36.15; 1906/7, 57.01; 1911/12, 61.49 [*RFAB* various years]. Therefore the major increase in revenue took place between 1896/7 and 1906/7, and within that period, between 1901/2 and 1906/7.
91. Mahit to Chulalongkorn, 11 May 1898, NA r5 Kh 14.1kh/8[g].
92. Mahit to Chulalongkorn, 21 December 1899, NA r5 Kh 14.1kh/12[g]; Mahit to Chulalongkorn, 12 December 1900, NA r5 Kh 14.1kh/15[g].
93. *RFAB* 1903/4, pp. 22–3.
94. Damrong to Chulalongkorn, 4 August 1903, NA r5 Kh 14.1kh/18[g].
95. Damrong to Sommot, 13 February 1904; Chulalongkorn to Damrong, 14 February 1904, NA r5 Kh 14.1kh/18[g].
96. Report on the meeting of the Council of Ministers, 15 December 1904, NA r5 Kh 14.1kh/18[g].

97. Ibid.
98. Memorandum containing proposals as to the manner in which revenue can be raised to supply the deficiency which will be caused by the abolition of gambling in the provinces, F. C. Giles, 7 January 1905, NA K Kh 0301.1.2/1; NA r5 Kh 14.1kh/18[g].
99. Ibid.
100. Mahit to Chulalongkorn, 9 January 1905, 16 January 1905; Report on the meeting of the Council of Ministers, 16 January 1905, NA r5 Kh 14.1kh/18[g].
101. Chulalongkorn to Devawongse, 18 January 1905, NA r5 Kh 14.1kh/18[g].
102. Prince Damrong, *Ru'ang tamnān kānlōekbǭnbia lae lōek huai* [The Abolition of Gambling Dens and the Huai Lottery], Bangkok, 1960, pp. 49–50.
103. Damrong to Sommot, 27 April 1906, NA r5 Kh 14.1kh/18[g].
104. Hamilton King [U. S. Minister in Bangkok] to Devawongse, 20 April 1905, NA r5 Kh 14.1kh/18[g].
105. *RFAB* various issues.
106. Strobel to Devawongse, 4 December 1905, NA r5 Kh 17.3/6.
107. Memorandum of a conversation between the Siamese Minister in Paris and M. Boissonnas [French Foreign Ministry], 22 February 1906: enclosed with Devawongse to Sommot, 12 April 1906, NA r5 Kh 17.3/6. Under the terms of its 1893 agreement with France, Siam was required to remove all her forces from the Cambodian province of Battambang. Thereafter the French government frequently applied diplomatic pressure on Siam to abandon all its claims over the province. This Siam did in 1907.
108. Minute attached to Raja Nuprabrandh [Siamese Minister in London] to Grey, 5 February 1906, PRO FO 371/131.
109. Memorandum: conversation with Mr. Strobel, Malay Peninsula railway, Campbell, 16 January 1907, PRO FO 371/385.
110. Strobel to Paget, 1 July 1907, PRO FO 371/331.
111. None of the records consulted in Bangkok offer an explanation why the government made no attempt to renegotiate the treaties as originally intended.
112. *RFAB* 1904/5, p. 7.
113. Čhanthaburī to Chulalongkorn, 30 January 1909, 22 February 1910, NA r5 Kh 14.2kh/10. [This was the reference when the documents were consulted in 1971–2].
114. Prince Damrong, *Ru'ang tamnān kānlōekbǭnbia lae lōek huai*, p. 51.
115. W. A. Graham, *Siam: A Handbook of Practical, Commercial and Political Information*, London, 1924, vol. 1, p. 340.
116. *RFAB* 1916/17, p. 5.
117. *RFAB* 1917/18, p. 3.
118. *Bangkok Times*, 29 May 1906.
119. For a detailed account of the establishment of the Book Club, Prince Mahit's central role in it, and the diplomatic dispute which preceded his resignation as Minister of Finance, see Ian Brown, *The Élite and the*

Economy in Siam c. 1890–1920, Singapore, 1988, chapter 4, particularly pp. 131–4.

120. Rivett-Carnac to Čhanthaburī, 31 March 1906, NA K Kh 0301.1.1/1; Mahit to Chulalongkorn, 18 April 1906, NA r5 Kh 5.1/25.

121. *Bangkok Times*, 6 June 1906.

122. *Rātchasakunwong* [Royal Genealogy], Bangkok, 1969; *Bangkok Times*, 16 April 1907.

5 The Ministry Disunited and Revived, 1906–10

The new Minister of Finance was Phrayā Suriyā, whose qualifications for the post were impressive. He was widely credited with the successful negotiation of the 1905 loan; he was fully familiar with modern financial practices; he had had ministerial experience, at the Ministry of Public Works from mid-1905. And the impressive welcome he had received from the King and the Council of Ministers on his return from Paris in 1905 would suggest that he was widely respected within the government. There was every indication that his term as Minister of Finance would be a success. In fact it was a failure. By January 1908, a mere eighteen months after his appointment, all but one of his major policies was either in ruins or facing severe criticism; he had greatly antagonized the King and Prince Damrong; his relationship with the Financial Adviser, Williamson, had deteriorated to a point beyond repair. Perhaps most seriously, by early 1908 Phrayā Suriyā had lost the confidence and cooperation of senior officials in his own ministry. However Phrayā Suriyā's period at the Ministry of Finance did contain one notable success, which it would be convenient to consider first. Appropriately it involved the scene of the Minister's earlier triumph – a European loan.

5.1 THE EUROPEAN LOAN OF 1907

When Phrayā Suriyā became Minister of Finance in June 1906, the government was already committed to raising a second loan in Europe.[1] By the beginning of the year 1906/7, only 3.713 million *baht* was left of the 14.5 million *baht* raised in 1905; yet in the 1906/7 budget inherited by Phrayā

Suriyā from Prince Mahit, 7.25 million *baht* had been allocated to railway construction, none of which was covered from current revenue.

The actual raising of the second European loan was a relatively straightforward matter. There was none of the debilitating hesitancy that had marked the government's approach to the first loan. The 1907 negotiations were complicated by just one factor – concern on the part of the British that Siam would use the proceeds of the loan to finance construction of the southern railway into the peninsula. There was fear in London and Singapore that either construction of that line would be placed in the hands of the German-dominated Siamese Railway Department or that German banks would succeed in underwriting a major part of the loan. In either case German influence in the peninsula could be expected to grow and rival that of Britain in that strategic area.

In August 1906 Phrayā Suriyā wrote to Axel Johnson asking for assistance in the negotiation of this second European loan, which was to be for £2 million.[2] When the British Minister heard that the loan was now to be negotiated, he sought assurances through Westengard (the acting General Adviser) that the construction of the peninsular line would be undertaken by either Siamese or British officials.[3] Westengard replied that the Siamese government had taken no decision contrary to the wishes of Britain. Negotiations with the European banks began in October. On this occasion the government was faced with a syndicate of the Hongkong and Shanghai Bank, the Banque de l'Indochine and the Deutsch-Asiatische Bank. The London and Paris banks had earlier agreed to join forces with the Berlin bank through fear that if they excluded the latter, the Deutsch-Asiatische would then offer more favourable terms to Siam and take the whole loan for itself.[4] Preliminary enquiries – conducted principally by Rivett-Carnac – produced an offer of $92\frac{1}{2}$ nett at $4\frac{1}{2}$ per cent, but Phrayā Suriyā preferred to wait until the market improved.[5]

However when Phrayā Suriyā reviewed the progress of the negotiations in a letter to the King on 7 December 1906, he admitted that the government could not delay too long.[6] By the end of the year, 31 March 1907, not only would the proceeds of the 1905 loan be exhausted but the Ministry of Finance would again be drawing on the treasury reserves to cover the allocation for railway construction. There was, Phrayā Suriyā continued, a further important consideration. In late 1902 the government had placed the *baht* on the gold-exchange standard.[7] Subsequently the currency had been repeatedly revalued in response to rises in the world price of silver. But at some point the government would wish to fix the *baht* against sterling. This would require the establishment of a gold/sterling fund, to enable the Siamese authorities to control short-term fluctuations in the *baht*/sterling rate. Phrayā Suriyā proposed that part of the proceeds of the forthcoming loan be set aside for that fund. It was therefore decided to increase the size of the loan from £2 million to £3 million.[8]

On 8 December 1906 the Siamese government's proposals were put to the Bangkok managers of the Hongkong and Shanghai Bank and the Banque de l'Indochine, representing all three banks in the syndicate.[9] The conditions attached to the 1905 loan would again apply, with the addition that the Siamese authorities would undertake to maintain the current exchange value of the *baht* against sterling. The banks were given three days in which to reply.[10] On hearing of these developments, the Foreign Office in London immediately contacted the Hongkong and Shanghai Bank to express its fear that part of the loan would be used to finance construction of the peninsular railway by the German-dominated Railway Department: the bank was asked to hold up the negotiations until an assurance had been obtained from the Siamese government on that point.[11] The British Minister, Beckett, saw Phrayā Suriyā on 9 December and Prince Devawongse the following day.[12] The Siamese ministers were not sure whether any of the proceeds of the loan would be devoted to the southern line. Westengard, whom Beckett saw later, doubted whether it would. It was clearly impossible for the British Minister to obtain firm assurances in the time available. The Foreign Office therefore accepted that the

Hongkong and Shanghai Bank could agree to the Siamese proposals, fearing that the Deutsch-Asiatische might leave the syndicate at any time and make a separate bid for the whole the loan.[13]

The negotiations were completed in the last days of December 1906. The terms were $93\frac{1}{4}$ nett at $4\frac{1}{2}$ per cent,[14] compared with $90\frac{1}{2}$ nett at $4\frac{1}{2}$ per cent for the 1905 loan. At the request of Phrayā Suriyā, the loan contract contained no reference to the use of part of the proceeds to support the *baht* exchange. The Minister would give an assurance on this point in a separate letter to the banks.[15] Before the Council of Ministers, Phrayā Suriyā emphasized that the government was providing the banks with only a general undertaking that part of the loan would be used to support the exchange: there would be no commitment with respect to the size of the proposed exchange fund or the rate at which the *baht* would ultimately be fixed.[16] The loan contract was signed in London on 19 January 1907.[17] Four banks underwrote the £3 million loan – the Hongkong and Shanghai Bank, the Banque de l'Indochine, (£1 million each), the Deutsch-Asiatische (£$\frac{3}{4}$ million) and a Scandinavian syndicate (£$\frac{1}{4}$ million),[18] the latter reflecting the role of a Scandinavian financier, Wallenberg, in the final negotiations. It was issued five days later, being oversubscribed four times.[19]

One final, general, point might be made about the 1907 loan, indeed about the 1905 loan as well. Throughout the negotiations the Siamese government attempted to minimize, indeed erase, the political implications of the loans. The most clear example of this was its refusal to consider any proposal which involved Siam in offering specific security (the completed sections of the railway or the customs revenue) or involved trade concessions (for example, with respect to the supply of railway materials). But the same principle was evident elsewhere: the use of a Scandinavian financier, a neutral, to assist in the final detailed negotiations rather than Rivett-Carnac; the decision in 1907 to provide a separate, general undertaking to the banks with respect to use of part of the loan to support the exchange rather than having a firm, precise commitment written into the loan contract.

Yet the loans remained very much a political issue. The most clear indication of that point was the unwillingness of the Siamese government in 1904 to negotiate with the Hongkong and Shanghai Bank alone while relations with France were strained. In effect, therefore, there was a strong tension between the wish of the Siamese administration to make the raising of a European loan a purely business transaction and the inescapable intrusion of political considerations. It was, of course, that tension that had been at the root of the deadlock in the Council of Ministers in 1903–1904.

The remaining major policies pursued by Phrayā Suriyā were, as noted earlier, considerably less successful. Indeed, within months of his appointment he began to attract criticism both from within and from outside the government: that criticism reached its climax in the first two months of 1908. I have considered Phrayā Suriyā's administration of the exchange and his abolition of the opium farm elsewhere.[20] There will be a brief reference to the fierce controversies generated by those policies when the Minister's resignation in February 1908 is considered. Here the focus will be on the regression of the Ministry of Finance's budgetary control under Phrayā Suriyā, not least because this will demonstrate perhaps his principal weaknesses – a tendency to antagonize ministerial colleagues and a proneness for precipitate action.

5.2 THE BUDGET AND AN ATTEMPT TO EXTEND FINANCIAL CONTROL, 1906–8

The budget for 1906/7, which covered almost the entire first year of Phrayā Suriyā's term as Minister of Finance, was inherited from Prince Mahit. Although the latter had been able to estimate for a small revenue surplus, the government's budget position was far from satisfactory. That small revenue surplus had been achieved, as was indicated earlier, only by charging the expenditure allocation for railway construction, some 7.25 million *baht*, to the loan account, which at the beginning of the year held just 3.713 million *baht*.[21] More importantly, while total revenue receipts had risen from 46.04 million *baht* in 1904/5 to 51.65 million *baht* in 1905/6, the estimates for 1906/7 allowed for an increase of only 1.7 million *baht* as compared with the previous year.[22] There were, in addition, specific areas for concern. The year 1906/7 was to see the closing of the last of the provincial gambling dens, and 1907/8 the closing of the dens in the capital, although alternative sources of revenue had been, or were being, prepared; crises in the opium and spirit farms in 1905 had not only threatened the immediate revenue but also made it clear that the major revenue farming syndicates were now dangerously unstable. The prospect of substantial budget deficits had, of course, been common in the early years of the decade, but Phrayā Suriyā faced a considerably more difficult situation than that which earlier had confronted Prince Mahit. The latter had been able, as a first line of defence, to draw on the reserves which had been built up in the late 1890s; by 1906 the reserves were very considerably reduced. Prince Mahit had enjoyed substantial increases in revenue receipts for almost every year in which he had had to prepare a budget; with Phrayā Suriyā, the period of rapidly rising revenues had clearly come to an end.

In these circumstances the first course for the Ministry of Finance was to examine whether the treasury was receiving the full value of the revenues. In late March 1906 Rivett-Carnac had written to Prince Čhanthaburī, then acting Minister of Finance during the illness of Prince Mahit, to point out that there was no effective accounting check on the revenues received from the kingdom's tax farmers.[23] The following month a European accountant employed in the Ministry of Finance, Ramsay, was given responsibility for checking those receipts,[24] and in October 1906 he submitted his first report.[25] Ramsay's investigations had uncovered a quite appalling state of affairs. At the end of August 1906 the total arrears of the tax farmers stood at 7.66 million *baht*. Out of a sum of 4.74 million *baht*, the arrears still owing for 1905/6, no less than 3.36 million *baht* was not covered by the security lodged by the farmers with the Ministry of Finance. Only about 16 per cent of tax farm payments were paid to the Ministry on time.

As a result of this report, Phrayā Suriyā increased the security demanded of the farmers and moved to impose interest charges on arrears.[26] But those modest measures, in themselves, could achieve little, and throughout Phrayā Suriyā's term as Minister the total arrears of the revenue farmers continued to grow, rising to 10.37 million *baht* in September 1907.[27] Over 90 per cent of arrears related to the years 1905/6 and 1906/7, and approximately 50 per cent were not covered by security.[28] Williamson viewed this situation with increasing dismay. In July 1907 he wanted the matter discussed by the Council of Ministers,[29] and in November he urged that it be reported to the King.[30] But the Financial Adviser's concern went unheeded. Phrayā Suriyā appears, quite simply, to have been unable to obtain more efficient administration from those of his officials with immediate responsibility in this matter.

And then his main policy for increasing the flow of revenues into the treasury stirred a fierce controversy with his ministerial colleagues. At the end of the 1890s, the creation of the Bangkok Revenue Department under the Ministry of the Capital and the Provincial Revenue Department under the Ministry of the Interior had absolved the Ministry of Finance almost completely of direct responsibility for the collection of those taxes which were collected by officials. Phrayā Suriyā did not want that function returned to his Ministry. But he did want to extend the influence of the Ministry of Finance over those collections. In December 1906 he wrote to Prince Damrong enclosing a copy of a letter from the King to Prince Mahit, written in February 1897, concerning the functions and responsibilities of the Ministry of Finance.[31] The King had confirmed the responsibility of the Ministry of Finance for the conduct of the government's financial administration and, now the important point, had confirmed the right of the Ministry to investigate without obstruction the work of other ministries and of the provincial administration that in any way touched on finance. On the authority of that letter, Phrayā Suriyā informed Prince Damrong, the *Krom Samruat*

[Investigation Department] of the Ministry of Finance would now undertake examinations of the financial work of the other ministries.

Prince Damrong complained to the King.[32] While he recognized the need for officials from the Ministry of Finance to carry out an audit of all parts of the administration, he was opposed to any attempt by Phrayā Suriyā to extend the Ministry's authority and control. Prince Damrong warned that if Phrayā Suriyā persisted, there was certain to be friction between the Ministry of Finance and the other ministries. A meeting between Prince Damrong and Phrayā Suriyā on 13 December 1906 aggravated the dispute.[33] Phrayā Suriyā explained that officials from the *Krom Samruat* would undertake periodic investigations of the revenue-collecting departments within the administration – principally the Provincial Revenue Department in the Ministry of the Interior. Prince Damrong replied that for relatively junior officials from the Ministry of Finance, with no practical experience of the administration of revenue collection, to investigate and criticize the work of more senior and experienced officials from the Ministry of the Interior could lead only to friction and to a decline in the efficiency and enthusiasm of those who were criticized. On 7 February 1907 Phrayā Suriyā again wrote to the King to argue that the *Krom Samruat* should be able to undertake more than a mere audit of the revenue collection accounts.[34] He pointed out, with some justification, that if a revenue official pocketed a part of the receipts (obviously leaving no record in the accounts), the *Krom Samruat*, if merely looking at the accounts, would not detect the fraud. The dispute between Phrayā Suriyā and Prince Damrong eventually came before the Council of Ministers, on 11 February 1907, but no solution was found.[35] It was suggested that Phrayā Suriyā prepare a more detailed outline of his proposals, and there the dispute was left to simmer.

The determination of the Minister of Finance to extend his authority over the revenue-collecting departments of the administration was prompted primarily by concern over the government's budget position. Phrayā Suriyā presented his first, indeed his only, budget to the King in March 1907.[36]

After achieving a revenue collection of 51.65 million *baht* in 1905/6 and budgeting for 54.7 million *baht* in 1906/7, the Ministry of Finance estimated revenue in 1907/8 at 50.7 million *baht*. For the first time since the government had introduced the modern form of budget in the early 1890s, the Ministry was expecting a fall in revenue. There were two main reasons for this pessimistic view. A poor monsoon in 1906, and consequently reduced rice exports in late 1906 and early 1907, meant cuts in the revenue estimates for the major tax farms, for land taxes, the customs and for railway traffic receipts, compared with the estimates for 1906/7.[37] Second Phrayā Suriyā argued that Prince Mahit's revenue estimates for 1906/7 had been far too optimistic, particularly with regard to the opium revenue. Moreover, in January 1907 the Ministry of Finance had abolished the opium farm and placed the monopoly under government administration. It would be unwise to assume that the opium revenue could be maintained in the first year of the new structure.

With regard to expenditure, the ministries had first submitted requests which totalled 65.76 million *baht*, but the Ministry of Finance had cut that back to 56.26 million *baht*. The result was an estimated revenue deficit of 5.56 million *baht* for 1907/8. On only one previous occasion, in 1901/2, had the government's published budget shown an expected deficit. In submitting his estimates to the King, Phrayā Suriyā made two points. He suggested that the Chinese poll tax be collected annually instead of triennially, as was the current practice. And, returning to his proposal to expand the authority of the *Krom Samruat*, he suggested that that Department, together with the Accounts Department of the Ministry of Finance, undertake a detailed examination of the expenditure of each ministry in an attempt to curb some alleged extravagances.

The estimates for 1907/8 and these two proposals came before the Council of Ministers on 19 March 1907.[38] The ministers accepted Phrayā Suriyā's proposal for the Chinese poll tax (it would be collected on an annual basis from 1908/9) but were far less enthusiastic with regard to his attempt to expand the authority of the Ministry of Finance over their expenditures. But the conflict between Phrayā Suriyā and his ministerial colleagues, in particular Prince Damrong, had to rest while the King left Siam on his second visit to Europe. On his return, the conflict came to a head. On 7 December 1907 Williamson submitted a long memorandum to Phrayā Suriyā on the current state of the government's finances.[39] It was a disturbing document. The Financial Adviser pointed out that during the course of 1907/8 the Ministry of Finance intended to withdraw 9.5 million *baht* from the treasury reserves, of which 5.5 million *baht* would be to cover the budget deficit for that year. This would leave only 14.5 million *baht* in the reserves at the beginning of 1908/9. Furthermore, there were clear signs that the government was heading for another budget deficit in 1908/9, of approximately 3.5 million *baht*, which would reduce the reserves to 11 million *baht*. Williamson continued:

> Without wishing to be at all alarmist, I feel it my duty to inform the Government that I regard the present position as one of considerable gravity, and unless a steady and combined effort is made for the next few years, the country may find itself in serious financial difficulties.[40]

The government had to impose much stricter control over its expenditure:

> As long as the revenue was expanding, we could afford to be more lenient to the demands of the departments, but the time has come, if we are to recover financial equilibrium without recourse to drastic measures, when the present rather extravagant tendencies must be firmly put a stop to.[41]

Williamson's memorandum was discussed by the Council of Ministers on 23 December 1907.[42] Surprisingly, Phrayā Suriyā did not attend. The discussion was dominated by Prince Damrong, who argued that attempts to cut the expenditure allocations of the ministries would lead only to a deterioration in the efficiency of the administration. Expenditure could be restrained only by reorganizing and rationalizing government departments. Then Prince Damrong turned on the Minister of Finance:

> Phrayā Suriyā has proposed that all the ministers be instructed to economize, to hold down expenditure. We hear this request every year but it never works because the ministers have no faith in the Minister of Finance. The reason for that is while the Ministry of Finance inspects and cuts the expenditure of all the other ministries, it does not inspect its own. Whatever it wants to spend, it spends. The expenditure of the Ministry of Finance is grossly extravagant. If the Ministry shared in the sacrifices of the other ministries, then government expenditure could be held down.[43]

The King then intervened. As Phrayā Suriyā was not at the meeting, the discussion would have to be held over.

But Prince Damrong maintained the pressure on the Minister of Finance. On 4 January 1908 he wrote to the King to request permission to appoint two additional inspectors in the Provincial Revenue Department to check the collection of revenue in the provinces.[44] By thus strengthening internal inspection, it could be said that Prince Damrong was attempting to block Phrayā Suriyā's ambitions. When Prince Damrong's request was discussed by the Council of Ministers, on 6 January, Phrayā Suriyā opposed the appointments.[45] But in so doing he came under criticism from the King himself, who suggested to him that his Ministry of Finance was finding it difficult to carry out its existing responsibilities with respect to the expenditure estimates. In particular, Chulalongkorn noted, the Ministry had found it impossible to examine in sufficient detail all the administration's requests for increases in salaries and positions. Furthermore, the King suggested, the other ministries were certain to oppose the close intrusion of the Ministry of Finance into their work, particularly as it was widely suspected that the Ministry would not impose the same parsimonious standards on itself as it sought to impose on others.

At that point Prince Damrong proposed the creation of a separate, independent, Inspection Department, with the authority to investigate suspected cases of extravagance and to determine salary rates and appointments across the administration. The idea was then developed by the King.[46] He proposed that the *Krom Samruat* and the *Krom Sārabānchī* [Accounts Department] be removed from the Ministry of Finance and established as a separate department. It would have the authority to examine the work of any ministry or department, and to discuss with departmental heads possible improvements in administration. It would be able to recommend that specific projects be commenced, hurried along or halted, depending on the availability of funds. It would have the right to cut the expenditure budget of a department where it was shown that the salary bill was excessive, and to increase the flow of funds to a department which had insufficient resources. Disputes between the proposed Inspection Department and a minister would be referred to the King.

If acted upon, these proposals would have emasculated the Ministry of Finance, reducing it merely to a storehouse for the kingdom's treasure. It seems certain that, in making them, the King and Prince Damrong were simply seeking to counter Phrayā Suriyā's attempts to push the authority of the Ministry of Finance over, beyond, the existing, pragmatically-determined, lines which divided responsibilities and functions between the ministries. When Phrayā Suriyā resigned, no more was heard of them.

5.3 THE RESIGNATION OF PHRAYĀ SURIYĀ, FEBRUARY 1908

In the final few months of his term as Minister of Finance, Phrayā Suriyā's position became increasingly embattled as he was forced to defend himself against driving criticism in the Council of Ministers. Between 23 December 1907 and 13 February 1908 Phrayā Suriyā attended no less than nine meetings of the Council at which he was heavily censured. The extreme hostility of the criticism can be judged from the following two passages. First, the King:

> The important point is not to pay attention to what Phrayā Suriyā says. He does not lie. But he lacks intelligence and discrimination. It is apparent that [his abilities] are below normal. If the revenue falls it is due to the lack of stability of Phrayā Suriyā rather than being the fault of anyone else. People despise the Minister rather than wish him harm. Because of his lack of stability, the Chinese feel contempt for him, officials in his own Ministry despise him. He is laughed at. He only trusts people who are not trustworthy. As a result the kingdom suffers a loss of revenue.[47]

And Prince Damrong: 'From what I have seen of the Ministry of Finance, no one will cooperate with Phrayā Suriyā. Furthermore, no one has faith in him – no one right through from the tax farmers to the Europeans.'[48]

In essence there were two criticisms of the Minister. The first was that he frequently pursued policies with an almost unreasonable determination, spurning the cooperation of colleagues and the assistance of subordinates and advisers. That trait could be seen in his insistent attempts to extend the authority of the Ministry of Finance over revenue collection throughout the kingdom, to the point of provoking the fierce opposition of Prince Damrong. There were other cases. In mid–1906 Phrayā Suriyā, ignoring the advice of Williamson, proceeded with a scheme to establish the *baht* as the principal currency in circulation in the southern province of Phuket, and thereby created a severe, if brief, *baht* shortage in the capital. In January 1907 he abolished the opium farm without effectively consulting the other ministries that would be involved – principally the Ministry of the Interior – as to the structure of government administration that was to replace it. He then worked towards a structure that would minimize the responsibility of the Ministry of the Interior in the administration of the monopoly outside the capital, to the great annoyance of Prince Damrong.[49] However the most damaging consequence of Phrayā Suriyā's determined insularity was not that he antagonized his ministerial colleagues but that he provoked hostility from his own senior officials. After a sharp exchange in October 1906 over the *baht* shortage, Williamson and the Minister appear to have maintained only a cool working relationship. More importantly, with respect to the government's administration of the opium monopoly, Phrayā Suriyā was soon in serious conflict with his principal official, Mọm Čhao Piya Phakdī. In time Phrayā Suriyā simply rode roughshod over the official's views: Mọm Čhao Piya Phakdī retaliated by ignoring the Minister's instructions. In short, the internal structures of the Ministry of Finance began to give way.[50]

The second major criticism of the Minister was that he lacked stability – that faced with a crisis he would panic. His decision to abolish the opium farm was hastily reached, his proposals for government administration of the monopoly were inadequately prepared and clumsily executed. During his term as Minister, Phrayā Suriyā pursued a revaluation of the *baht* (against the advice of Williamson) which, taking place as it did during a sharp trade depression, was, at the very least, ill-timed.

After the last of the meetings of the Council in early 1908 at which these and the other miscalculations and shortcomings of the Minister of Finance were explored, Phrayā Suriyā received a letter from the King:

> I can see that the Ministry of Finance is in considerable difficulties…It is disunited and the Minister is making mistakes. Subordinate officials are doing no work. The Minister has no expertise in the work of his Ministry; therefore everything that he does is really just an experiment - he proceeds by trial and error. Outsiders think that he does not have the authority to control the Ministry…matters which should cause no difficulty, cause difficulty; problems which should not arise, arise. It is apparent that the Minister

is ignorant of his work and that his stability is doubted by everyone... Because of these shortcomings [in the Minister] the government's revenue has fallen greatly, and there have been considerable difficulties with the budget.[51]

But the King acknowledged that Phrayā Suriyā had achieved much in his earlier posts, principally as Siamese Minister in Paris. There was now a danger that those successes would be obliterated by the current run of failures.

Therefore I think that I must give you a confidential warning... If you feel that you cannot bring unity [to the Ministry] and cannot correct your mistakes, then you would be advised to leave the Ministry and take up some other work... I am giving you this advice with kindness and with the hope that I can help you in the future.[52]

The final paragraphs of the King's letter were almost consoling, but Phrayā Suriyā could not have mistaken the main thrust. The following day he left the Ministry of Finance.[53]

The reasons for Phrayā Suriyā's failure as Minister of Finance are complex and difficult to unravel. It must be acknowledged that he had considerable ill-fortune. He arrived at the Ministry of Finance just as the period of rapid expansion in the revenues was coming to a close. The longer-term problems of the revenue were intensified, in the immediate prospect, by the poor monsoons of 1906 and 1907. Within six months of Phrayā Suriyā taking office, the syndicate administering the government's major source of revenue, the opium monopoly, collapsed, and the Minister was faced with the problem of bringing that huge operation under government administration.[54] With regard to the exchange, it was Phrayā Suriyā's misfortune that he had to deal first with a sharp rise in the price of silver and then, from early

1907, with a dramatic fall, and at a time when the rice export trade was depressed. These were very considerable difficulties.

They overwhelmed the Minister of Finance. In a letter written on the day he resigned, Phrayā Suriyā explained to Chulalongkorn how he had virtually lost control of the problems which faced his Ministry:

> I had been at the Ministry of Finance for only a few days when I could see what a tremendous amount of work there was to do. There were numerous deficiencies in the administration which I had to try to rectify... yet I was constantly having to deal with trifling matters, so that I had insufficient time to deal with the more important problems facing the Ministry. It was then my misfortune that all the major problems came to a head at the same time and I could not find time to consider each of them carefully.[55]

Phrayā Suriyā described the difficulties he had had in coping with each crisis – the *baht* shortage in late 1906, the collapse of the opium farm:

> When these problems were arising I remained silent – hesitated to inform you – because I feared that you would be displeased and would take it as a sign that I was disheartened with my work and was about to give up.[56]

It is possible that this reluctance to confide his fears and difficulties was a major factor in Phrayā Suriyā's increasingly insular behaviour. And perhaps important in this context was the fact that Phrayā Suriyā was a member of the Bunnag family. His father was Phrayā Montrīsuriyāwong (Chum Bunnag), who had been head of the Royal Pages Corps earlier in the reign, and his grandfather was Somdet Čhao Phrayā Bǫrommahāprayūrawong (Dit Bunnag), the head of the *Kalāhōm* from 1830 to 1851 and head of the *Phra Khlang* from 1822 to 1851.[57] He was a nephew of the ex-regent. Yet when Phrayā Suriyā became Minister of Finance in 1906, eight of the twelve ministerial positions were held by members of the royal family, and of the four non-royal ministers, all except Phrayā Suriyā occupied relatively less important positions – at Agriculture, Public Instruction and Public Works.[58] Holding a crucially important post in a Council of Ministers dominated by the royal family, Phrayā Suriyā was encouraged in his insularity. Certainly, once things began to go wrong he found it extremely difficult to seek the assistance he so clearly needed from the inner circles of the Council, and in particular from the King. The last quotation above can be interpreted as an admission of that. Thus increasingly Phrayā Suriyā pursued his own policies, rejected the views of his advisers, avoided discussion with ministerial colleagues and even his own senior officials.[59]

5.4 THE APPOINTMENT OF THE NEW MINISTER OF FINANCE, PRINCE ČHANTHABURĪ, FEBRUARY 1908

The resignation of Phrayā Suriyā left the Ministry of Finance in a most demoralized condition. Not since the mid-1890s, with first the resignation of Prince Narāthip and then the two lifeless ministries of Prince Narit and Prince Sirithat Sangkāt, had it been so lacking in authority. The Ministry even found its internal disunity a topic for discussion in the editorial columns of the *Bangkok Times*.[60]

It took the Council of Ministers almost two hours to reach a decision on the appointment of a new Minister of Finance.[61] It is significant that the King wished to appoint a member of a noble family, for, he explained to the Council, if Phrayā Suriyā were to be succeeded by one of his own brothers or sons, it would appear that the departing Minister of Finance had been driven from office by royal design. But the Council could think of no official of noble birth who could fill the position. The King then suggested that Prince Devawongse be moved from the Ministry of Foreign Affairs to the Ministry of Finance. But who would replace Prince Devawongse? Eventually the Council of Ministers moved towards one of the King's sons, Prince Čhanthaburī. Born in 1874, he had gone to England in 1885, as part of the first group of Chulalongkorn's sons to be educated abroad.[62] On his return to Siam in 1895 he had been appointed Director-General of the Education Department. In April 1902 he had become Controller-General in the Ministry of Finance, the position he held on the resignation of Phrayā Suriyā in February 1908. He had had one short spell as acting Minister of Finance – in early 1906 when ill-health had forced Prince Mahit to take leave. However in early 1908 the King was reluctant to promote Prince Čhanthaburī to this position in his own right, for he felt that his son as yet lacked the authority to hold his own in the thrust and turmoil of high-level administration.[63] Perhaps the King was influenced by memories of Prince Čhanthaburī's rather undistinguished record as head of the Education Department.[64] But Prince Čhanthaburī had the strong support of Prince Damrong. It was eventually agreed that Prince Čhanthaburī would be appointed acting Minister of Finance for a trial period, during which time Prince Narit, Minister in 1893–1894, would exercise a general supervision over his work.[65] But by the end of March Prince Čhanthaburī had proved his ability, and from 1 April 1908 he was confirmed as Minister of Finance,[66] the first of Chulalongkorn's sons to reach ministerial rank.

As it turned out, the King need not have been concerned about his son's abilities. Prince Čhanthaburī became one of the most distinguished and perhaps the most powerful Minister of Finance in the period of the late absolute monarchy. He remained at the Ministry until January 1923, a period of almost fifteen years. However the present work will be concerned with just his first two years at the Ministry – which will take the study to the end of the reign of King Chulalongkorn in 1910 – and it will focus on the budget problems faced by the new Minister.[67]

5.5 BUDGET PROBLEMS, 1908–10

Most of the groundwork on the 1908/9 budget had been completed by Phrayā Suriyā before he resigned. That budget was submitted to the King by Prince Čhanthaburī on 16 March 1908.[68] The new Minister drew attention to a number of issues which were to be fully discussed over the following two years. First, he pointed out that the army and navy, which had accounted for just over 10 per cent of total government expenditure in 1901/2, had taken 23 per cent of total expenditure in 1907/8. Prince Čhanthaburī wanted no expansion in the army and navy allocations for at least five years. Second, Prince Čhanthaburī noted a further reduction in the expenditure of the Irrigation Department, indicating that the government was moving towards a final rejection of a large-scale irrigation initiative. Third, with respect to the northern railway, there was concern that the segment between Phitsanulok and Nakon Sawan could not be profitable, because it traversed a commercially poor region.[69] This raised the question whether the administration should halt construction south of Chiangmai, at least until the government's financial position had improved. At the meeting of the Council of Ministers on 23 March 1908 it was decided that the Minister of Public Works would undertake an investigation of the profitability of the northern railway above Nakon Sawan.[70]

However the most important point now made by Prince Čhanthaburī concerned the division between the three main categories of government expenditure – ordinary expenditure (salaries and administrative expenses); extraordinary expenditure (for example, on the purchase of materials for public works projects, on the purchase of military equipment); and special expenditure (for example, the allocation for the Privy Purse, stipends for the Lao chiefs, payments made in connection with the European loans). In the 1908/9 estimates, ordinary expenditure accounted for 71 per cent of the total, extraordinary expenditure for 7 per cent, and special expenditure for 22 per cent. It was clear, Prince Čhanthaburī argued, that a disproportionate share of the revenue was being devoted to salaries and administrative expenses. This was an old problem. In the late 1890s it had led to the creation of the Committee on Establishments. The following two years were to show just how deep-seated that problem was.

In 1909/10, ordinary expenditure again absorbed by far the major part of the revenues: it accounted for 44.82 million *baht* or 71 per cent of total expenditure.[71] Extraordinary expenditure, which had been severely cut the previous year, was again cut, down to 3.75 million *baht* in 1909/10 from 4.41 million *baht* in 1908/9. The ministries' original requests for extraordinary expenditure in 1909/10 had come to a total of 9.44 million *baht*. It was clear that the increases in the government's revenue were being swallowed up by increasingly larger allocations for salaries and administrative expenses, leaving a diminishing proportion of the government's resources for special and extraordinary expenditures. At the same time, Prince Čhanthaburī warned, there were certain to be unavoidable increases in the latter over the coming years, not least because repayments on the 1905 sterling loan would begin in 1909/10.

There was therefore an extremely strong case for restraint in government expenditure, particularly in ordinary expenditure. Prince Čhanthaburī put forward a number of proposals. He repeated his call for a restriction on military expenditure, suggesting that the Ministry of War be allocated no more than 25 per cent of total government expenditure over the coming five years. Second, he reported that at a meeting attended by himself, Čhao Phrayā Thēwēt (the Minister of Agriculture), Williamson and the Dutch irrigation engineer, van der Heide, it had been decided, after many years of discussion, to abandon all plans for a large-scale irrigation initiative.[72] And finally, Prince Čhanthaburī confirmed a decision already taken by the administration – to halt construction of the northern railway just beyond Uttaradit, a point which the Railway Department expected to reach by November 1910.

But these cuts in the expenditure allocations for the military, irrigation and the railway, severe as they were, did not confront the major problem – the very high proportion of revenue resources being absorbed by official salaries and expenses. That issue was tackled by the King when the 1910/11 budget came before the Council of Ministers, in May 1910.[73] The root of the problem lay, Chulalongkorn argued, with the unwillingness of the Siamese to make their living in commerce or business. The ambition of the overwhelming majority of Siamese was to find employment in government service. The pre-reform administration had been able to absorb vast numbers, largely because no salaries were paid. Officials had been expected to make their living by *kin mu'ang* – by retaining a portion of the revenues which passed through their hands, and by prizing payments from the people for tasks performed. With the reform of the administration from the late 1880s those circumstances had greatly changed. By introducing a mass of regulations (particularly financial regulations) to govern the bureaucratic behaviour of officials, the opportunities for *kin mu'ang* had been reduced: and by paying salaries to officials, the need to *kin mu'ang* had been, in theory, obviated. It was clear, the King continued, that once the government began to meet the costs of running the administration directly, it became extremely difficult for it to absorb large numbers of new recruits without drastically reducing the allocation of resources to important projects and initiatives.

This problem was accentuated by several other factors. In the pre-reform administration it had been common for a department to engage considerably more officials than its work required. This practice had been carried over into the reformed administration, with the result, the King argued, that every ministry had a substantial corps of officials who had little or no work, yet who still drew a government salary.[74] Second, in the reformed administration, salary levels were high, partly because the government had been forced to employ a large number of European officials who demanded to be paid well (and the government would not wish to discriminate in this respect between its European and Siamese employees), partly because, as the Siamese were reluctant to make their living from commerce, families whose men had government positions were usually entirely dependent on that salary. What was really needed, Chulalongkorn argued, were changes of attitude: for the Siamese to look upon commerce and business as acceptable ways of making a living and to stop regarding government service as the only honourable, secure source of employment; for the administration itself to cease appointing large numbers of lower-grade officials for whom frequently it had no particular work. In May 1910 it was agreed that each minister would impose a 3 per cent cut in his ordinary expenditure, to be secured mainly by dismissing redundant staff, and would then conduct a thorough examination of the functions and staff-levels of his administration in an attempt to improve efficiency.[75] But this was an ineffectual response to a very deep-seated problem. In March 1924, Williamson would write:

> For a good many years past, there has been a tendency for the expenditures to consist more and more of salaries and contingencies while the allotments for extraordinary expenditures, i.e. administrative public works and the like, have now been curtailed to a minimum. The position, therefore, now is that it is almost impossible to economize expenditures in any way which was possible fifteen years ago, by making heavy cuts in the extraordinary grants in order to meet the necessity for economy which has arisen. The budget consists now to so large an extent of *kan pracam* (i.e. ordinary or current) items, that there is practically no scope for reductions....unless the tendency is checked there will be a danger of nearly the whole of the disbursements of the government consisting of salaries and contingencies – leaving practically nothing for permanent works, whether of a developmental or administrative character.[76]

Notes

1. Mahit to Phrayā Suriyā, 1 June 1906, NA r5 Kh 3/2.
2. Phrayā Suriyā to Johnson, 27 August 1906, NA K Kh 0301.1.25/3.
3. Foreign Office, London: Memorandum on the proposal of the Siamese Government to construct a railway in the Siamese Malay Peninsula, and

the suggested publication of the Secret Convention with Siam of 1897, 31 December 1906, Printed, PRO FO 371/385.

4. Memorandum: interview with Mr. Townsend of the Hongkong and Shanghai Bank, Campbell, 19 October 1906, PRO FO 371/182.
5. Rivett-Carnac to Phrayā Suriyā, 23 October 1906, 2 November 1906; Phrayā Suriyā to Rivett-Carnac, 8 November 1906, NA K Kh 0301.1.25/3.
6. Phrayā Suriyā to Chulalongkorn, 7 December 1906, NA r5 Kh 25/9.
7. See Ian Brown, 'Siam and the Gold Standard, 1902–1908', *Journal of Southeast Asian Studies*, 10, 2 (September 1979), pp. 381–99.
8. Phrayā Suriyā to Chulalongkorn, 7 December 1906, NA r5 Kh 25/9.
9. Beckett to Grey, 19 December 1906, with enclosures, PRO FO 371/385.
10. Townsend [London office of the Hongkong and Shanghai Bank] to Campbell, 11 December 1906, PRO FO 371/182.
11. Minutes attached to, Townsend to Campbell, 10 December 1906, PRO FO 371/182.
12. Beckett to Grey, 12 December 1906, PRO FO 371/182; Beckett to Grey, 19 December 1906, with enclosures, PRO FO 371/385.
13. Townsend to Campbell, 11 December 1906, PRO FO 371/182.
14. Bangkok managers of the Hongkong and Shanghai Bank and the Banque de l'Indochine to Phrayā Suriyā, 31 December 1906, NA K Kh 0301.1.25/3.
15. Bangkok manager of the Hongkong and Shanghai Bank to Williamson, 29 December 1906, NA K Kh 0301.1.25/3.
16. Report on the meeting of the Council of Ministers, 31 December 1906, NA r5 Kh 25/8.
17. Phrayā Wisut to Devawongse, 19 January 1907, NA r5 Kh 25/9.
18. Townsend to Campbell, 31 December 1906, PRO FO 371/182.
19. Phrayā Wisut to Devawongse, 24 January 1907, NA r5 Kh 25/9.
20. Ian Brown, 'Siam and the Gold Standard, 1902–1908', *Journal of Southeast Asian Studies*, 10, 2 (September 1979), pp. 381–99; Ian Brown, 'The End of the Opium Farm in Siam, 1905–07', in John Butcher, Jennifer Cushman and Howard Dick (eds.), *The Rise and Fall of Revenue Farming in South-East Asia*, London [forthcoming].
21. *RFAB* 1906/7, pp. 3, 9.
22. Ibid., pp. 1–3.
23. Rivett-Carnac to Čhanthaburī, 31 March 1906, NA K Kh 0301.1.1/1. Rivett-Carnac was acting Financial Adviser while Williamson was on leave in Europe.
24. Čhanthaburī to Mọm Anuwongse, 5 April 1906, NA K Kh 0301.1.1/1.
25. Memorandum: inspection of the Chao Cham Nuan accounts, Williamson, 31 October 1906, NA K Kh 0301.1.1/1.
26. Phrayā Suriyā to Chulalongkorn, 27 December 1906, NA r5 Kh 14/27; Memorandum: revenue farms, Williamson, 26 December 1906, NA K Kh 0301.1.1/1.
27. Memorandum: revenue farms arrears, Williamson, 30 November 1907, NA K Kh 0301.1.1/1.

28. Memorandum: arrears of revenue farms, Williamson, 6 July 1907, NA K Kh 0301.1.1/1.
29. Ibid.
30. Memorandum: revenue farms arrears, Williamson, 30 November 1907, NA K Kh 0301.1.1/1.
31. Damrong to Chulalongkorn, 6 December 1906, NA r5 Kh 1/44.
32. Ibid.
33. Damrong to Sommot, 14 December 1906, NA r5 Kh 1/44.
34. Phrayā Suriyā to Sommot, 7 February 1907, NA r5 Kh 1/44.
35. Report on the meeting of the Council of Ministers, 11 February 1907, NA r5 Kh 1/44.
36. Phrayā Suriyā to Chulalongkorn, March 1907, NA r5 Kh 5.1/25.
37. *RFAB* 1907/8, pp. 4–8.
38. Report on the meeting of the Council of Ministers, 19 March 1907, NA r5 Kh 5.1/25.
39. Note by the Financial Adviser on the present financial position in Siam, Williamson, 7 December 1907, NA r5 Kh 5.1/25; NA K Kh 0301.1.30/8.
40. Ibid.
41. Ibid.
42. Report on the meeting of the Council of Ministers, 23 December 1907, NA r5 Kh 5.1/25.
43. Ibid.
44. Damrong to Chulalongkorn, 4 January 1908, NA r5 Kh 14.1/7.
45. Report on the meeting of the Council of Ministers, 6 January 1908, NA r5 Kh 1/45.
46. Note by Chulalongkorn, January 1908, NA r5 Kh 1/44.
47. Report on the meeting of the Council of Ministers, 3 February 1908, NA r5 Kh 14.1kh/28.
48. Report on the meeting of the Council of Ministers, 13 February 1908, NA r5 Kh 26/15.
49. Phrayā Suriyā's policies with respect to the exchange and the opium monopoly are considered in Ian Brown, 'Siam and the Gold Standard, 1902–1908', *Journal of Southeast Asian Studies*, 10, 2 (September 1979), pp. 381–99; Ian Brown, 'The End of the Opium Farm in Siam, 1905–07', in John Butcher, Jennifer Cushman and Howard Dick (eds.), *The Rise and Fall of Revenue Farming in South-East Asia*, London [forthcoming].
50. In his autobiography *Fū'n khwām lang* [Reviving the Past], Bangkok, 1967–1968, Anuman Rajadhon refers to an incident in which Phrayā Suriyā apparently antagonized one of his most senior officials. It appears that Phrayā Suriyā ordered the dismissal of an official in the Customs Department without informing the director of that department, Prince Phrǫm. Prince Phrǫm subsequently resigned.
51. Chulalongkorn to Phrayā Suriyā, 14 February 1908, NA r5 Kh 3/2.
52. Ibid.
53. Phrayā Suriyā to Chulalongkorn, 15 February 1908, NA r5 Kh 3/2.
54. Here it might be noted that one source suggests that in fact the King allowed, perhaps encouraged, Phrayā Suriyā to resign in order to quell the fierce protest that had come from the opium farmers in response to the

Minister's abolition of the farm: biography of Phrayā Suriyānuwat, included in the third (1975) printing of his *Saphasāt*, p. 15. See note 59 below.

55. Phrayā Suriyā to Chulalongkorn, 15 February 1908, NA r5 Kh 3/2.
56. Ibid.
57. *Lamdap rātchinīkun bāng chāng* [Genealogy of the Royal Maternal Line 'Bāng Chāng'], 2nd. ed., Bangkok, 1919; David K. Wyatt, 'Family Politics in Nineteenth Century Thailand', *Journal of Southeast Asian History*, 9, 2 (September 1968), pp. 208–28; Akin Rabibhadana, *The Organization of Thai Society in the Early Bangkok Period, 1782–1873*, Ithaca, 1969, Appendix F and pp. 200–1.
58. David K. Wyatt, 'The Beginnings of Modern Education in Thailand, 1868–1910', PhD diss., Cornell University, 1966, Appendix A.
59. Phrayā Suriyā did not return to government service until 1926. In 1911 he published the first modern economics text in Thai, *Saphasāt* [The Science of Wealth]. Strongly influenced by the nineteenth century British socialist tradition, this work had a major impact on the generation of Thai political economists which came to the fore in the mid-1970s. See Chatthip Nartsupha, 'The Economic Thought of Phraya Suriyanuwat', in Vichitvong na Pombhejara (ed.), *Readings in Thailand's Political Economy*, Bangkok, 1978, pp. 402–13; Ian Brown, 'Economic Thought in Early Twentieth Century Siam', in Manas Chitakasem and Andrew Turton (eds), *Constructions of Thai Knowledge*, London, 1991, pp. 84–98.
60. *Bangkok Times*, 27 February 1908.
61. Report on the meeting of the Council of Ministers, 17 February 1908, NA r5 Kh 3/2.
62. David K. Wyatt, *The Politics of Reform in Thailand. Education in the Reign of King Chulalongkorn*, New Haven, 1969, pp. 148, 180–1, 296.
63. Report on the meeting of the Council of Ministers, 17 February 1908, NA r5 Kh 3/2.
64. Wyatt, op. cit., pp. 267–92, 295–6.
65. *Bangkok Times*, 20 February 1908, 21 February 1908.
66. Chulalongkorn to Čhanthaburī, 24 March 1908, NA r5 Kh 3/2.
67. For Prince Čhanthaburī's work in finally fixing the value of the *baht* against sterling, see Ian Brown, 'Siam and the Gold Standard, 1902–1908', *Journal of Southeast Asian Studies*, 10, 2 (September 1979), pp. 381–99.
68. Čhanthaburī to Chulalongkorn, 16 March 1908, NA r5 Kh 5.1/26.
69. Report on the meeting of the Council of Ministers, 23 March 1908, NA r5 Kh 5.1/26.
70. Ibid.
71. Čhanthaburī to Chulalongkorn, 17 March 1909, NA r5 Kh 5.1/27.
72. Ibid. For a detailed consideration of the administration's irrigation proposals and decisions in the 1900s, see Ian Brown, *The Élite and the Economy in Siam c.1890–1920*, Singapore, 1988, chapter 1.
73. Report on the meeting of the Council of Ministers, 6 May 1910, NA r5 Kh 5.1/28.

74. One explanatory point must be added. The King's fears concerned the large number of low-grade officials who had, and needed, little training. The argument should not obscure the fact that the government suffered from a serious shortage of well-educated, capable officials in the higher levels of the administration.
75. Report on the meeting of the Council of Ministers, 6 May 1910, NA r5 Kh 5.1/28.
76. Memorandum, Williamson, 27 March 1924: quoted in Stephen L. W. Greene, 'Thai Government and Administration in the Reign of Rama VI (1910–1925)', PhD diss., University of London, 1971, pp. 393–4

6 Assessment and Perspectives

The central theme that has sustained the preceding chapters is that of the newly-established modern Ministry of Finance seeking to project an increasing authority over the finances of the Siamese administration in the final two decades of the reign of King Chulalongkorn. Clearly that process did not proceed altogether smoothly – indeed quite the reverse, particularly in the early years. Yet there is a firm contrast between the clumsy and obdurate manner in which Prince Narāthip compiled the expenditure estimates in the early 1890s and the ordered manner in which they were drawn up by Prince Čhanthaburī at the end of the 1900s; and a firm contrast between the detailed accounts of the government's finances published in the *Report of the Financial Adviser on the Budget* again at the end of the 1900s and the distressing ignorance on the part of the Ministry of Finance of many of the details of ministerial expenditure during the terms of Prince Narit and Prince Sirithat Sangkāt in the mid-1890s. Even so, at the close of Chulalongkorn's reign there remained substantial inadequacies in the Ministry's exercise of financial control, important weaknesses in its authority. The opening part of this concluding chapter will explore this point.

6.1 ASSESSMENT

Attention must first be drawn to the extreme weakness of the Ministry's audit procedures. The 1890 legislation which formally established the Ministry of Finance made no provision for a department charged exclusively with carrying out audits of the administration's accounts, although that may have been part of the responsibilities of the *Krom Truat* [Investigation Department]. Even at the beginning of the reign of King Vajiravudh (1910–25), the administration still lacked a clearly defined audit department.[1] As a result, although the Ministry of Finance would draw up detailed estimates of the future expenditures of the ministries and would ensure that each ministry and department drew only its sanctioned allocation from the treasury, it could not ensure that those withdrawals were used strictly in accordance with the sanctioned estimates. In brief, the Ministry lacked firm control over the actual expenditures of the administration.[2] Two illustrations will support the point. In a memorandum written in December 1907, Williamson pointed out that departments commonly transferred any funds which they had accumulated (usually secured under the provisions for salaries and administrative expenses) to projects and initiatives which had failed to attract allocations from the Ministry of Finance when the expenditure estimates had been set.[3] Departments were thus financing schemes which had not been agreed with the Ministry of Finance, and subsequently sanctioned by the Council of Ministers. Second, it would appear that in the early 1910s most ministries and departments still maintained accounts with the Bangkok banks.[4] This implied either that they were failing to use their expenditure allocation immediately it was drawn from the treasury or that they were neglecting to remit to the Ministry of Finance all revenues collected under their administration. By so developing concealed sources of funds – individual treasuries, in the manner of the pre-reform administration – the ministries were able to avoid close scrutiny of their actual expenditures by the Ministry of Finance. The Ministry's authority and control were undermined. The installation of effective audit procedures would have curbed those practices.

It is not evident from the documentary record why, in this period, those procedures were in fact so weak. Undoubtedly one consideration was that there was a shortage of appropriately trained and experienced officials to monitor the cash flows of the administration. But it is also possible that in this period ministers were in fact unwilling to see the emergence of an effective audit department, precisely because that would have enabled the Ministry of Finance to achieve a strict control over their expenditures. This is an important point to which the argument will return.

If there were substantial inadequacies in the Ministry's control over expenditures, its control over the administration's revenues was far more seriously flawed. The latter reflected the emergence by the mid-1890s of an increasingly powerful Ministry of the Interior, taking control, in the manner of the pre-reform administration, of a growing range of governmental functions outside the capital. The important development here was the creation of the Provincial Revenue Department within the Ministry of the Interior in 1899, foreshadowed by the establishment of the Bangkok Revenue Department within the Ministry of the Capital the previous year. At the end of the reign of Chulalongkorn, those two departments were responsible for the collection of about one-third of the administration's total revenue.[5] As the Ministry of Finance had no control over the collection of such a substantial proportion of the government's revenue, its control over the administration's finances as a whole was inevitably weakened. Unable to command directly all the revenues raised in the kingdom, it could not firmly command the administration's expenditure. The practice referred to earlier, of ministries and departments each maintaining accounts with the banks in Bangkok, has some significance here. In the mid-1910s it was noted that commonly the revenue departments outside the Ministry of Finance were still placing a proportion of their revenue receipts in those accounts rather than transferring them directly, in full, into the treasury.[6] That practice would again enable those departments, or the parent ministry, to proceed with initiatives which the Ministry of Finance had refused to sanction. The latter, with far from complete control over the revenues, inevitably had incomplete control over expenditure.

In a broader sense too, the emergence of a powerful Ministry of the Interior by the mid-1890s inhibited the growth of the Ministry of Finance. With government and administration dominated by Prince Damrong and his Ministry, it was extremely difficult for any Minister of Finance to exert a powerful authority. Two examples will illustrate the point. It required the persistent intervention of the King in support of Prince Mahit at the end of the 1890s to ensure that all ministers, including prominently the Minister of the Interior, firmly acknowledged the authority of the Ministry of Finance in the processes by which the annual expenditure estimates were compiled. Second, when Phrayā Suriyā, attempting to exert a stronger control over the revenues, proposed that the Ministry of Finance would examine the revenue collections carried out by the Provincial Revenue Department, he was fiercely repulsed by Prince Damrong. And it must also be noted that Prince Damrong was to the fore in attacking the troubled Phrayā Suriyā in the closing weeks of his term as Minister of Finance.

It follows that for the Ministry of Finance to establish a stronger authority, at the very least the domination of the administration long exercised by the Ministry of the Interior would need to come to an end. This occurred within a few years. Following the resignation of Prince Damrong in 1915, the Provincial Revenue Department and the Bangkok Revenue Department were removed from the Ministry of the Interior and the Ministry of the Capital and reallocated within the Ministry of Finance. There they were combined and renamed simply the *Krom Sanphākǫn* [Revenue Department].[7] The collection of virtually all revenues now became the direct responsibility of the Ministry of Finance. That same year also saw the creation, at last, of an audit department [*Krom Truat Ngoen Phāendin*] within the Ministry of Finance, and a strengthening of the Ministry's accounting procedures by the amalgamation of the *Krom Sārabānchī* and *Krom Truat* into a *Krom Bānchīklāng*.[8]

But despite that advance, it is clear that the Ministry of Finance, then and later, fell some considerable way short of dominating the, centrally important, financial core of government. In this context it is important to note the views of a foreign economic adviser to the Thai government on the place of the Ministry of Finance within the administration's budget procedures in a later period – the mid-1950s. The adviser's views were quoted in Fred W. Riggs, *Thailand: The Modernization of a Bureaucratic Polity*:

> The Finance Ministry for its part does not have, in practice, the authority to rule out some projects altogether in order to permit other more important projects to be done adequately and at an adequate developmental pace. Hence the Finance Ministry's Budget Committee is necessarily reduced to 'nibbling' at the requests for funds emanating from other Ministries. No executive officer has antecedently made the more drastic decisions to accept or reject certain projects *in toto*. The Finance Ministry has no authority to do so.[9]

Riggs would explain that position in terms of his bureaucratic polity model. Where administration priorities and decisions reflected primarily the outcome of internal bureaucratic competition and conflict, a powerful financial division, whether embodied in the Ministry of Finance or in some other office, would fail to emerge.[10] Indeed such a division – determining the allocation of resources across the administration – would not be permitted to emerge, for it would thereby possess an overwhelming advantage on the bureaucratic battle field. It may be possible to interpret the position of the Ministry of Finance in the final two decades of the reign of King Chulalongkorn in terms of the same model. Where priorities and decisions reflected almost exclusively the contrasting administrative weights of ministers and ministries, the Ministry of Finance would not be allowed to achieve a dominating authority. Thus in the period covered by this study, the other ministries yielded somewhat reluctantly to the procedures laid down by the Ministry of Finance for the setting of the annual expenditure estimates; were quite prepared to assume responsibility themselves for the collection of a major part of the revenues; shifted surplus allocations to unauthorized initiatives, held back revenues and maintained accounts at banks in the capital, all with the aim of circumventing the agreed expenditure allocations; and failed to encourage (on at least one occasion, actively resisted) the establishment of structures and procedures by which the Ministry of Finance would conduct an effective audit of their financial flows.

The discussion above has focused on the position of the Ministry of Finance within the reformed administration. But brief reference must also be made to the Ministry's attempts in this same period to instil new concepts of financial propriety across the administration – to wean officials away from the practices and behaviour associated with *kin mu'ang*. The reference must indeed be brief, for there is no primary evidence here from which an assessment might be made. However there may be good reasons to suggest that the Ministry's efforts in this respect were not notably successful – apart from the obvious point that those earlier forms of administrative behaviour, or variations of them, have continued to thrive in Thailand in more modern times. First, there could be little hope of the Ministry of Finance successfully implanting the new concepts of financial propriety throughout the administration – primarily by the issue of volumes of regulations and directives – if it did not also institute an effective audit of the vast revenues and expenditures now handled by officials at all levels. Second, an important consequence of the reform of the government structure initiated from the end of the 1880s and of the reforms subsequently promoted by each of the new ministries was that the population of Siam was now faced with a notably more intrusive and pervasive administration. In their daily lives, the people came increasingly into contact with provincial administrators, tax assessors and collectors, police and judicial officials. And as those contacts increased, then surely the opportunities for squeeze grew. It is difficult to accept that the regulations and directives of the Ministry of Finance would have made great headway in those circumstances.

6.2 PERSPECTIVES

The assessment above of the achievements of the Ministry of Finance in its first two decades might well be too severe. With the evidence available it is simply not possible to determine the extent to which the other ministries continued to retain revenues, and in this and other ways, were able to circumvent the expenditure estimates 'agreed' with the Ministry of Finance. Neither is it possible to determine whether, in this period, officials across the administration in fact faced expanding or contracting opportunities to exercise the practices associated with *kin mu'ang*. Moreover, it may be unreasonable to have anticipated that the Ministry of Finance, in the brief period covered by this study, would have achieved more than it did in effecting such major reform. Indeed it might be felt that it did well to get so far. But far more importantly, the assessment above may be built on an inappropriate premise. Assessment must be set in the context of aim and objective. What were the aims and objectives of the reform of the government administration undertaken in Siam in the final two decades of the reign of Chulalongkorn, and what was to be the place of the new Ministry of Finance in meeting them? Those broad questions are the focus of the remaining pages of this study: and it requires, as an initial step, a return to the study's opening pages.

There reference was made to King Chulalongkorn's statement, in a letter to Prince Damrong in January 1896, of the case for reform in terms of the threat posed by the European powers which now, with increasing menace, surrounded the kingdom. If that threat were to be countered it was essential that the government maintain a high level of order and stability within the borders of the kingdom, so that foreign intervention be neither encouraged or provoked. And that required the creation of an administrative structure that would secure the effective government of the kingdom, even in its furthest extremities. The tasks of the Ministry of Finance within that strategy, and they were crucial to the strategy's success, were to see that the revenue was sufficient to finance the schemes, projects and general administration of a government with a growing range and burden of responsibilities, and to allocate the resources it commanded in pursuit of effective administration. But it is possible to interpret Chulalongkorn's reform of the government administration in a quite different manner – to see it in terms of a sharp consolidation of the political and administrative power of the King himself.[11] An outline of this argument also appeared in the opening chapter. From the early part of the nineteenth century, control of the major ministries had commonly been held by members of the Bunnag family. The influence of that family had reached its height during the opening years of Chulalongkorn's reign when, as the King was a minor when he came to the throne, Čhao Phrayā Sī Suriyawong, then the head of that family, occupied the position of regent. During that period the Bunnags restricted still further the flow of revenues to the King and his family, and several princes found themselves in serious financial difficulties. Denied resources, drained of political and administrative power, Chulalongkorn was fiercely determined to restore the authority of his position. He threw himself recklessly into this task at the end of his minority, and was repulsed. He then proceeded, methodically, securely, as the major reform of government administration was initiated towards the end of the 1880s. The place of the Ministry of Finance in this strategy, again crucial, is surely clear: it was to secure the revenues for the King.

Two points might be made about these strategies, apart from the fact that they were not mutually exclusive. First, during the reign of Chulalongkorn, and beyond, they were successful. The establishment of a centralized structure of provincial administration, the modernization of the armed forces and the construction of a railway network radiating from the capital, secured internal peace and order: external intervention was not provoked, sovereignty was maintained. The reform of the government administration, the political advancement of the King's brothers and then his sons, the growing centralization of the administration's finances, secured royal power. By the end of Chulalongkorn's reign, the degree of authority exercised by the absolute monarchy – over the administration and over the kingdom – was unprecedented. The Ministry of Finance played a full role in both strategies. Second, in important respects, both strategies implied only a limited measure of reform. This applies in two senses. Where change was undertaken, it was commonly of a limited nature. The army was reformed – new methods of recruitment were introduced, modern training practices were developed, modern equipment was purchased – but only to the point where that force would be able to maintain internal order.[12] It was not anticipated that the modernized army would be able to confront a powerful external aggressor, or indeed that it should become aggressive itself beyond the borders of the kingdom. The centralization of the administration's finances proceeded to the point where the government's (modest) initiatives could be funded. It was not anticipated that the Ministry of Finance would impose an iron grip on the revenues and expenditures of the government. But the second sense is the more important. The reform undertaken by Chulalongkorn from the late 1880s was limited in the sense that there were substantial areas where little or no change was attempted.[13]

It would be easier to approach this argument by the assertion that Chulalongkorn's reforms did not seek fundamental change in the social, economic or political structures of the kingdom. Neither strategy noted earlier – that of reform being a response to an external threat, that of reform being the instrument to secure a royalist consolidation – required it. Indeed fundamental change threatened both strategies, and particularly the latter. That assertion is most vividly illustrated by the reforms in education. Those did not seek to produce, by heavy investment in a modernizing education system, the trained labour-force that would be demanded by an industrializing economy and, at the élite level, the large corps of highly-educated, innovative individuals, drawn from a wider range of socio-economic origins, that would take command of a vital, modernizing bureaucracy. In 1911, of nearly 1 000 000 boys between the ages of 6 and 14 years, only 85 000 were attending elementary and primary schools, and a further 210 000 were receiving some form of instruction in the monasteries.[14] There was no university in Siam prior to the establishment of Chulalongkorn University in the mid-1910s. Universal education, even at the elementary level, was not achieved until after 1940. The contrast here is with Japan. Japan would challenge the west, an ambition that demanded fundamental social, economic and political change: Siam would accommodate it, with minimum disturbance to the established order.[15]

With that perspective it would be inappropriate to seek in the Ministry of Finance of this period a driving force for radical change. Indeed, would it be harsh to suggest that when the Ministry did take an important initiative in these years – placing the *baht* on the gold-exchange standard, placing the great revenue monopolies under direct government administration – in essence it was forced by circumstances to do so: in the examples here, by the long depreciation of silver against gold, by the collapse of the great farming syndicates? The essential task of the newly-established Ministry of Finance was to secure a measure of command over the kingdom's revenues, a measure of command over the government's expenditures. It achieved that task well. It was required to do little more.

Notes

1. Stephen L.W. Greene, 'Thai Government and Administration in the Reign of Rama VI (1910–1925)', PhD diss., University of London, 1971, p. 50.
2. Therefore the possibility must be admitted that the ministries were more willing to accept the budget allocations set for them because they knew that those estimates could be circumvented. This is an important observation which will be taken up later.
3. Note by the Financial Adviser on the present financial position in Siam, Williamson, 7 December 1907, NA K Kh 0301.1.30/8; NA r5 Kh 5.1/25.
4. Memorandum, Williamson, 21 July 1914, NA K Kh 0301.1.29.B/13.
5. Statistics of the Provincial Revenue Department r.s. 121–133 (1902/03–1914/15), NA K Kh 0301.1.1/4; Čhao Phrayā Yommarāt to Chulalongkorn, 1 December 1909, NA r5 Kh 14.1/7.
6. Regulation issued by the Minister of Finance regarding the keeping of banking accounts by government departments, May 1914, NA K Kh 0301.1.29.B/13. However it must be admitted that the records give no indication of the scale of the ministries' bank accounts, no indication of the extent to which revenues were retained and not submitted directly to the treasury. This point is taken up later.
7. Wichai Prasangsit, *Prawatsanphākǭn* [History of Taxation], Bangkok, 1971, pp. 338 – 9.
8. Ibid., pp. 332–8; Greene, op. cit., p. 239.
9. Fred W. Riggs, *Thailand. The Modernization of a Bureaucratic Polity*, Honolulu, 1966, p. 332.
10. Ibid., particularly pp. 329–38.
11. For a statement of this view, Benedict R. O'G. Anderson, 'Studies of the Thai State: The State of Thai Studies', in Eliezer B. Ayal (ed.), *The Study of Thailand: Analyses of Knowledge, Approaches, and Prospects in Anthropology, Art History, Economics, History, and Political Science*, Athens, Ohio, 1978, pp. 193–247.
12. See Noel Alfred Battye, 'The Military, Government and Society in Siam, 1868–1910: Politics and Military Reform during the Reign of King Chulalongkorn', PhD diss., Cornell University, 1974.
13. 'The role of the Jakri dynasty, if modernizing, was modernizing only in the special sense that the regimes of colonial governors were modernizing.' Anderson, op. cit., p. 199.

14. David K. Wyatt, *The Politics of Reform in Thailand. Education in the Reign of King Chulalongkorn*, New Haven, 1969, pp. 373–5.
15. For further consideration of this point, Ian Brown, *The Élite and the Economy in Siam c.1890–1920*, Singapore, 1988, pp. 178–80.

Select Bibliography

MANUSCRIPT SOURCES

(a) National Archives of Thailand (NA)

(i) Royal Secretariat

[Krom Rātchalēkhāthikān]: these records cover the period from the reform of government administration which began in the late 1880s to the end of the absolute monarchy in 1932. They comprise the administrative correspondence between the King (or his secretary) and the ministers, reports on meetings of the Council of Ministers, administrative notes and drafts made either by the King or his secretary, and copies of correspondence between and within ministries where these had been sent to the Royal Secretariat. Almost all the records from this collection which were consulted for this study came from a single series, that is the series from the fifth reign, the reign of Chulalongkorn [r5] concerned with the Ministry of Finance [Kh]. In addition, a few documents were consulted from the series, again from the fifth reign, concerned with miscellaneous matters [B]. These records were by far the most important source for this study. When they were consulted, in 1971 and 1972, the National Archives was located in a part of the old National Library, in the grounds of *Wat Mahāthāt*, close to the Grand Palace.

(ii) Office of the Financial Adviser

[Samnakngān Sēthakit Kānkhlang]: these are the records of the British Financial Advisers. They carry the prefix: K Kh 0301.1. When these records were consulted, in 1971 and 1972, they were held in the Library of the Ministry of Finance, then just within the main gate of the Grand Palace. In their later move to the new National Archives, some minor reclassification took place. In revising this study for publication, every effort has been made to cite documents from this collection by their present, National Archives, references.

(iii) Ministry of Agriculture

[Krasuang Kasētrāthikān]: these records of the Ministry carry the prefix: KS.

(b) Public Record Office, London (PRO): the records consulted for this study were Foreign Office records (FO) in the five series 17, 69, 371, 628 and 633.

NEWSPAPERS

Bangkok Times (weekly, 1887–1890; semi-weekly, 1891–1894; thrice weekly, 1894–1895; daily, 1896–1941)
Rātchakitčhānubēksā [Royal Gazette] (weekly, 1858–1859, 1874–1879, 1888–)
Siam Repository (quarterly, 1869–1874)
The Times (daily)

DISSERTATIONS

BATTYE, NOEL ALFRED (1974) 'The Military, Government and Society in Siam, 1868–1910: Politics and Military Reform during the Reign of King Chulalongkorn', PhD diss. (Cornell University).
BROWN, IAN GEORGE (1975) 'The Ministry of Finance and the Early Development of Modern Financial Administration in Siam, 1885–1910', PhD diss. (University of London).
GREENE, STEPHEN L.W. (1971) 'Thai Government and Administration in the Reign of Rama VI (1910–1925)', PhD diss. (University of London).
HOLM, DAVID F. (1977) 'The Role of the State Railways in Thai History, 1892–1932', PhD diss. (Yale University).
NEON SNIDVONGS (1961) 'The Development of Siamese Relations with Britain and France in the Reign of Maha Mongkut, 1851–1868', PhD diss. (University of London).
WYATT, DAVID K. (1966) 'The Beginnings of Modern Education in Thailand, 1868–1910', PhD diss. (Cornell University).

PRINTED WORKS

AKIN RABIBHADANA (1969) *The Organization of Thai Society in the Early Bangkok Period, 1782–1873*, Southeast Asia Program, Data Paper 74 (Ithaca, New York: Cornell University).

ANDERSON, BENEDICT R.O'G (1978) 'Studies of the Thai State: The State of Thai Studies', in Eliezer B. Ayal (ed.), *The Study of Thailand: Analyses of Knowledge, Approaches, and Prospects in Anthropology, Art History, Economics, History, and Political Science*, Center for International Studies, Southeast Asia Series 54, pp. 193–247 (Athens, Ohio: Ohio University).

ANUMAN RAJADHON (1967–8) *Fū'n khwām lang* [Reviving the Past] (Bangkok: Su'ksit Sayām).

ANUMAN RAJADHON (1939) *Tamnān sunlakākǫn* [History of the Customs Department] (Bangkok: cremation volume).

BRAILEY, NIGEL (1989) *Two Views of Siam on the Eve of the Chakri Reformation: Comments by Robert Laurie Morant and Prince Pritsdang* (Whiting Bay, Arran: Kiscadale Publications).

BROWN, IAN, 'British Financial Advisers in Siam in the Reign of King Chulalongkorn', *Modern Asian Studies*, 12, 2, pp. 193–215 (April 1978).

BROWN, IAN (1991) 'Economic Thought in Early Twentieth Century Siam', in Manas Chitakasem and Andrew Turton (eds.), *Constructions of Thai Knowledge* (London: School of Oriental and African Studies).

BROWN, IAN, 'Siam and the Gold Standard, 1902–1908', *Journal of Southeast Asian Studies*, 10, 2, pp. 381–99 (September 1979).

BROWN, IAN (1988) *The Élite and the Economy in Siam c.1890–1920* (Singapore: Oxford University Press).

BROWN, IAN (forthcoming), 'The End of the Opium Farm in Siam, 1905–07', in John Butcher, Jennifer Cushman and Howard Dick (eds), *The Rise and Fall of Revenue Farming in South-East Asia* (London: Macmillan).

CARTER, A. CECIL (1904) *The Kingdom of Siam* (New York: G.P. Putnam's Sons).

CHALŌEM YONGBUNKŌET, 'Ngoenkū khrangrāek khǫng prathētthai' [Thailand's First Loan], *Wārasān krombanchīklāng*, May 1961, pp. 43–51.

CHATTHIP NARTSUPHA (1978) 'The Economic Thought of Phraya Suriyanuwat', in Vichitvong na Pombhejara (ed.) *Readings in Thailand's Political Economy* (Bangkok: Bangkok Printing Enterprise) pp. 402–13.

CHULALONGKORN, KING (1927) *Phrarātchahatlēkhā phrabāt somdet phra čhunlačhǫmklao čhaoyūhua song thalāeng phraborommarātchāthibāi kāekhai kānpokkhrǫng phāendin* [King Chulalongkorn's Speech Explaining the Changes in the Government], (Bangkok: commemorative volume).

DAMRONG RAJANUBHAB, PRINCE (1923) *Phraprawat somdet phračhao borommawongthōe krom phrayā thēwawong warōpakān* [Biography of Prince Devawongse] (Bangkok: cremation volume).

DAMRONG RAJANUBHAB, PRINCE (1963) *Ru'ang laksana kānpokkhrǫng prathētsayām tāe borān* [The Old System of Government in Siam] (Bangkok).

DAMRONG RAJANUBHAB, PRINCE (1960) *Ru'ang tamnān kānlōekbǫnbia lae lōek huai* [The Abolition of Gambling Dens and the Huai Lottery], (Bangkok: cremation volume).

DAMRONG RAJANUBHAB, PRINCE (1963) 'Tamnān phāsī ākǫn bāngyāng' [The History of Some Taxes], in *Latthi thamniam tāngtāng* [Various Customs] (Bangkok: Khlang Witthayā), pp. 143–264.

DAMRONG RAJANUBHAB, PRINCE (1967) *Thēsāphibān* [The *Thēsāphibān* System of Provincial Administration] (Bangkok: cremation volume).

GRAHAM, W. A. (1924) *Siam: A Handbook of Practical, Commercial and Political Information*, 3rd ed. (London: Alexander Moring).

HALL, D. G. E. (1968) *A History of South-East Asia*, 3rd ed. (London: Macmillan).

INGRAM, JAMES C. (1971) *Economic Change in Thailand 1850–1970* (Stanford: Stanford University Press).

Lamdap rātchinīkun bāng chāng [Genealogy of the Royal Maternal Line 'Bāng Chāng'] 2nd ed. Bangkok: cremation volume (1919).

LE MAY, R. S. (1932) *The Coinage of Siam* (Bangkok: The Siam Society).

MINISTRY OF FINANCE (1931) *Krom phra čhanthaburī mu'a damrong tamnāeng sēnābǫdī krasuang phrakhlang* [Prince Čhanthaburī as Minister of Finance], (Bangkok).

MINISTRY OF FINANCE (annually from 1901/2) *Report of the Financial Adviser on the Budget of the Kingdom of Siam* (Bangkok).

NARITSARĀNUWATTIWONG, PRINCE (1963) *Banthu'k ru'ang khwāmrū tāngtāng* [Notes on Various Knowledge]: correspondence between Prince Narit and Phraya Anuman Rajadhon (Bangkok: Social Science Association of Thailand).

NORMAN, SIR HENRY (1895) *The Peoples and Politics of the Far East* (London: T. Fisher Unwin).

NORMAN, SIR HENRY, 'Urgency in Siam', *Contemporary Review*, 64 (1893), pp. 737–48.

PRIVY PURSE DEPARTMENT (1967) *Prawat samnakngān phra khlang khāngthī* [History of the Privy Purse Department] (Bangkok).

Rātchasakunwong [Royal Genealogy] (1969) (Bangkok: cremation volume). Edited by Prince Damrong Rajanubhab.

RIGGS, FRED W. (1966) *Thailand. The Modernization of a Bureaucratic Polity* (Honolulu: East-West Center Press).

ROYAL STATE RAILWAYS, *Report on the Traffic of the Royal Siamese State Railways*, from 1897/8, [title varies].

SAINT-HUBERT, CHRISTIAN DE, 'Rolin-Jacquemyns (Chao Phya Aphay Raja) and the Belgian Legal Advisers in Siam at the turn of the Century', *Journal of the Siam Society*, 53, 2, pp. 181–90 (July 1965).

SĪ SAHATHĒP (n.d.) *Raya thāng sadet phrarātchadamnōen praphāt prathēt yurōp r.s. 116* [The Royal Tour of Europe in 1897] (Bangkok).

SIFFIN, WILLIAM J. (1966) *The Thai Bureaucracy. Institutional Change and Development* (Honolulu: East–West Center Press).

SKINNER, G. WILLIAM (1957) *Chinese Society in Thailand: An Analytical History* (Ithaca, New York: Cornell University Press).

SUPHĀPHǪN ČHARANPHAT (1980) 'Phrayā Suriyānuwat nai kitčhakānfin khǫng rathabān' [Phrayā Suriyānuwat and Government Administration of the Opium Monopoly], in Sirilak Sakkriangkrai (ed.), *Phrayā Suriyānuwat (Koet Bunnāk) naksētthasāt khonrāek khǭng mu'ang thai* [Phrayā Suriyānuwat (Koet Bunnāk): Thailand's First Economist] (Bangkok: Thai Watthanā Phānit), pp. 165–81.

SURIYĀNUWAT, PHRAYĀ (1975), *Saphasāt* [The Science of Wealth] (Bangkok: Samnakphim Phikkhanēt).

TEJ BUNNAG, 'Khabotngiao mu'angphrāe r.s. 121' [The 1902 Shan Rebellion at Phrāe], *Sangkhomsāt parithat*, 6, 2, pp. 67–80 (September–November 1968).

TEJ BUNNAG (1977) *The Provincial Administration of Siam 1892–1915. The Ministry of the Interior under Prince Damrong Rajanubhab* (Kuala Lumpur: Oxford University Press).

THAMMASAT UNIVERSITY (1971) *Nangsū' ānprakǭp khambanyāi wichā phū'nthān ārayatham thai* [Handbook on Basic Thai Culture] (Bangkok).

VAN DER HEIDE, J. HOMAN (1903) *General Report on Irrigation and Drainage in the Lower Menam Valley* (Bangkok: Ministry of Agriculture).

WALES, H.G. QUARITCH (1934) *Ancient Siamese Government and Administration* (London: Bernard Quaritch).

WICHAI PRASANGSIT (1971) *Prawatsanphākǭn* [History of Taxation] (Bangkok).

WIRA WIMONITI (1961) *Historical Patterns of Tax Administration in Thailand* (Bangkok: Institute of Public Administration, Thammasat University).

WOOD, W.A.R. (1926) *A History of Siam* (London: T. Fisher Unwin).

WYATT, DAVID K., 'Family Politics in Nineteenth Century Thailand', *Journal of Southeast Asian History*, 9, 2, pp. 208–28 (September 1968).

WYATT, DAVID K. (1984) *Thailand. A Short History* (New Haven: Yale University Press).

WYATT, DAVID K. (1969) *The Politics of Reform in Thailand. Education in the Reign of King Chulalongkorn* (New Haven: Yale University Press).

Index